Expect!
Engage!
Empower!

Expect! Engage! Empower!

Three Pathways to Powerful Learning

Laurie Barron

Patti Kinney

ConnectEDD Publishing

Hanover, Pennsylvania

This publication is available at discount pricing when purchased in quantity for educational purposes, promotions, or fundraisers. For inquiries and details, contact the publisher at: info@connecteddpublishing.com

Published by ConnectEDD Publishing LLC
Hanover, PA
www.connecteddpublishing.com

Cover Design: Kheila Casas

Expect! Engage! Empower! —1st ed. Paperback
ISBN: 979-8-9933701-3-2

Praise for *Expect! Engage! Empower!*

Fair warning: If you are a building leader who misses the classroom or a classroom practitioner looking to re-ignite the fires that brought you to teaching in the first place, get ready to feel that wonderful tug at the best parts of your educator selves. There is a keen professionalism expected of educators in *Expect! Engage! Empower!* that is missing in many other education books these days. Yes, a lot is expected of teachers and building leaders in today's schools, especially as we enter the middle portion of the 21st century, but Laurie Barron and Patti Kinney provide specific tools to make it happen. And what a powerful dynamic: Two clearly experienced and knowledgeable school leaders who are also deeply practical and effective with classroom instruction and the research behind it—There might just be something to this idea of principals as instructional leaders! I come to these pages for candid insights, inspiration, real classroom examples, active learning strategies, behind-the-scenes leadership, and ample research, and I stay for the authentic agency the ideas provide students, teachers, and their leaders. Empowered indeed!

—Rick Wormeli | Author, Speaker, and Consultant

Expect! Engage! Empower! offers a clear, practical framework for creating classrooms where all students can thrive. Grounded in research and practice, it challenges educators to raise expectations, design meaningful and engaging learning experiences, and build student ownership in lasting ways. What makes this book valuable is its balance of inspiration and action. It affirms the potential of every learner and also provides concrete strategies to make that belief visible every day. This book is essential for educators and leaders committed to transforming learning into a truly impactful experience.

—Todd Whitaker | Research Professor, Presenter, and Author

By focusing on teacher beliefs, active involvement, and student ownership, *Expect! Engage! Empower!* offers practical strategies for anyone committed to equipping students with the confidence and skills they need to thrive in both school and life.

> —Eric Sheninger | Former Award-winning Principal, Best-Selling Author, and Global Consultant

If you're questioning how to truly reach every student while maintaining high standards, *Expect! Engage! Empower!* by Laurie Barron and Patti Kinney offers the clarity you've been looking for. This book goes beyond inspiration, delivering a practical framework that helps educators raise expectations, deepen engagement, and build real student ownership. Barron and Kinney skillfully bridge research and practice, showing exactly how powerful learning takes shape in today's classrooms. If you want strategies that actually move the needle for students, this book is for you.

> —Glenn Robbins | Award-Winning Educational Leader, Best-Selling Author, and Speaker

Even in the face of today's changes and challenges from within and outside of school setting, great educators still create learning opportunities and environments to equip students with competencies that enable them to thrive now and in the future. Laurie and Patti offer a unique avenue to such powerful learning for students by entwining a focus on attainment of high expectations with intrinsic engagement and true student empowerment. They remind us that now, more than ever, students need such approaches as substantive feedback, purposeful peer interaction, deep thinking, compelling content, challenging work, and a sense of belonging. Dive into their fresh trove of practical strategies, personal insights, and real-life examples—all ready to be put to work helping you, your school, and your classroom become places of powerful learning.

> —Jack Berckemeyer | Author, Speaker, and Humorist

There is a lot of outside noise that can distract teachers from their core purpose: ensuring students learn at high levels. But Laurie Barron and Patti Kinney have written a book that brings us back to the heart of education. *Expect! Engage! Empower!* is grounded in research yet written with the warmth of two experienced educators who never lost their passion for kids. It's an important addition to the toolkit for any teacher wanting to improve their craft.

—Danny Steele | Author, Speaker, and former principal

Do we believe all students can succeed? If so, how do we move from belief to action? *Expect! Engage! Empower!* offers a roadmap for creating conditions where all students can succeed, translating compelling ideas into practical implementation by focusing on high expectations, meaningful engagement, and student empowerment. This book offers a guide for transforming our classrooms into spaces where students believe in themselves and can truly thrive.

—Katie Powell | Director for Middle Level Programs, Association for Middle Level Education

Expect! Engage! Empower! is a compelling and practical read that challenges educators and leaders to rethink how expectations, relationships, and voice shape success. With a clear focus on connection and intentional practice, the book offers timely insights and real-world strategies that inspire meaningful engagement and lasting impact. It's both motivating and actionable—a powerful reminder that when we expect more, engage intentionally, and empower fully, people rise.

—Kim Campbell | Dean of Students, Hopkins, MN

This book clearly captures the essential elements of student learning. It emphasizes that strong relationships and a sense of belonging are the foundation, meaningful engagement is essential, and helping students recognize their potential is the ultimate goal. It's a valuable resource for new leaders and a helpful reminder for experienced leaders to stay focused on what matters most.

> —David Law | Superintendent, Minnetonka Public Schools and AASA President 2025-2026

If we want to truly move the needle on high expectations, engagement, and empowerment, those things can't just live in a single classroom or gather dust in a PD folder. As Laurie Barron and Patti Kinney so powerfully argue, they must be deeply embedded in every "corner of the school." What I love about this book is that it's not just theory; it's a masterclass in the "how." They've provided an incredible framework of real-world stories, actionable strategies, and mantras that an entire school community can actually live by. I was especially fired up by the specific scripts and wording they provide throughout the framework, tools that *any* staff member can use with colleagues and students to shift the cultural needle. I am 100% using this book in our school to raise expectations, engage every stakeholder, and empower everyone to build the kind of culture that eats strategy for breakfast!

> —Jon Konen | Superintendent, Author, and Consultant

Barron and Kinney present a well-constructed framework grounded in established research and enriched by thoughtfully integrated personal narratives drawn from their extensive professional experience. This work offers valuable insights for educators in a multitude of roles, from aspiring teachers to experienced administrators, supporting the development of practices which foster a culture of powerful learning outcomes for students. It serves as an excellent resource for lesson planning, systematic problem-solving, and the design and implementation of district-wide professional development.

> —Tobin Novasio | Former Superintendent

Barron and Kinney remind us what's possible when we truly believe in every learner. Grounded in real-world experience as teachers, leaders, and change agents, this book cuts through the noise with a clear, actionable framework: Expect. Engage. Empower. When expectations rise, students discover what they're capable of. When we engage students deeply, learning comes alive with purpose and meaning. And when we empower students, they grow into confident, capable individuals ready to shape their own futures. This is the playbook for educators who are serious about transforming learning for every student, every day.

—Todd L. Brist | Principal and Author

What sets this book apart is the unmistakable authenticity behind every page. These are not theorists but veteran practitioners who have walked the walk as teachers, principals, and district leaders, and it shows in the specificity and honesty of their guidance. Every chapter is a gift to educators, pairing compelling stories with concrete strategies that can be adapted to every setting and student. This is an essential read for anyone who believes that powerful learning is every child's right.

—Stephanie Simpson | CEO, Independent Educational Consultants Association (IECA)

Student motivation crucially depends on engagement in the school or classroom climate through participation. This book clearly breaks down the necessary steps to help students engage deeper not only in the academic components but also in the climate.

—Nathan Maynard | Internationally Best-Selling Author and Leading Authority in Discipline

Expect! Engage! Empower! Three Pathways to Powerful Learning by Dr. Laurie Barron and Patti Kinney is more than a book, it's a blueprint for transformation in today's classrooms. From the very first pages, the authors redefine *power* not as control, but as capacity. The capacity for students to think deeply, act purposefully, and own their learning journey. This isn't theory sitting on a shelf; it's practical, research-aligned, and rooted in what moves the needle in schools. What makes this work stand out is the clarity of its framework: Expect. Engage. Empower. These strategies are a call to action for every educator who refuses to settle for compliance when transformation is possible. If you raise expectations without raising support, you create pressure, but when you raise both, you create power, because engagement isn't just a strategy, it's the evidence that learning has meaning. Dr. Don Parker's perspective? As the author of *Building Bridges* and *Be the Driving Force Leading Your School on the Road to Equity*, this book speaks my language. It centers relationships, student voice, and real-world relevance while pushing educators to be intentional, strategic, and unapologetic about excellence. If you're serious about building bridges and a culture where students don't just learn, but become, this book belongs in your hands and in your professional learning communities. This is how we move from teaching lessons to transforming lives.

—Don Parker | Education Speaker and Author

In my eighteen years as a district superintendent across the unique landscapes of rural, midsize, and large urban systems, I have seen first-hand that powerful learning does not happen by accident. It happens when we intentionally choose to expect the best, engage the heart, and empower the individual. In Expect! Engage! Empower!, Laurie Barron and Patti Kinney provide a rare gift to our profession by blending hard research with the kind of deep, heartfelt wisdom that can only come from the front lines of education. This book offers the tools to move beyond the status quo and build a culture where every child knows they belong and believes they can succeed. It is honest, hopeful, and exactly what our schools need right now.

—Dr. LaTonya M. Goffney - Superintendent, Aldine ISD

Table of Contents

Part I: Expect!

Part II: Engage!

Part III: Empower!

Foreword

There's a kindergarten classroom in Washington state on a Native American reservation. For years, the students' data ranked toward the bottom, with the lowest test scores in the district and among the lowest in the state. That was until *one thing fundamentally shifted*. Within eighteen months, these students' data moved from the bottom of the state to the top. Students from the reservation were outperforming students at some of the most affluent schools in the Seattle suburbs. Not because anything external changed. Not the teacher. Not the curriculum. Not the families' resources. Not the students' abilities. But because an adult looked at those five-year-olds, shifted perspective, and decided something different: *that their brains could grow.* That struggle meant progress. That they weren't "fixed;" they were just "not yet" where they needed to be. With that, everything changed. Not because the kids became smarter. But because *they began to believe they could* become smarter. Because an adult believed it first.

Carol Dweck tells this story in her research on growth mindset. It's backed by what she also discovered working with 10-year-olds early in her career. She gave them problems that were slightly too difficult. Some students froze: "I hate this. I'm not good at this." But others lit up. One said, "I love a challenge." The difference? Those students had been taught that struggle was a sign their brains were growing. That resistance meant progress. That "not yet" was an invitation to believe they could succeed, not a dead end.[1]

A decade-long study tracked 15,000 tenth graders. Researchers asked teachers one simple question: "How far in school do you expect this student to get?" Years later, they followed up. The students whose teachers expected them to finish college? Most of them did. They graduated, built stable lives, and needed less public assistance as adults.[2] *Teachers' expectations literally helped shape students' futures.* Not just whether they passed the test. Whether they went to college. Whether they became economically independent. Whether they believed in themselves enough to build a life full of aspirations.

John Hattie spent years examining and synthesizing more than 2,100 meta-analyses comprising more than 132,000 studies involving 300 million students around the world. He was hunting to find what matters most for student achievement.[3] He found many student and school factors with positive effects. At the top of the list? *What teachers believe a student can do* (teacher estimates of achievement) What else? *Collective teacher efficacy* (when teachers believe together that they can make a difference for all students).[4]

So, what's the common denominator in the three stories above? *Belief drives everything.*

In my twenty-five years in education, I've walked through hundreds of classrooms. I've sat with teachers who love their jobs. Those who stay up late grading and show up daily with a genuine heart. Yet many of them, consciously or not, hold lower expectations for some students than others. Not because they're bad people. Because the systems we've inherited make it easier. Because we all carry biases. Because it's simpler to maintain the status quo.

The gap between what we say we believe about students and what students actually experience can be enormous. Students take in everything. Which students get called on. Whose work gets amplified. Whether an adult believes in them. What we believe about them. They feel it in the thousand small moments. The eye contact. The time taken. The questions asked. The feedback given. When expectations are low, even quietly, students internalize the message. They lower their own expectations. They disengage. Over time, they believe it, and their lives follow that belief.

Yet, there's hope. Research consistently shows what happens when we get it right. When teachers genuinely expect students to succeed and communicate that belief through their actions, questions, support, and time, *students become what's expected of them.* The kindergarteners went from the bottom to the top. The tenth graders whose teachers believed in them went to college. And across all the data, the pattern remains the same: *belief transforms outcomes.*

So how do we intentionally harness that power? How do we move from hoping students will succeed to systematically and deliberately creating the conditions in which success becomes inevitable? How do we shift from random acts of high expectations to a culture where *every student, every day,* knows that adults believe in them?

That's what this book is about. Laurie Barron and Patti Kinney haven't written this from theory. They've lived it as teachers, administrators, and system-changers who've walked the walk. They've seen what works and have distilled it into three pathways that are simple in names but robust in their contributions to powerful learning for students: *Expect. Engage. Empower.*

Expect. Not in some hollow way, but genuinely. Believing in students' capacity and communicating that belief through personalized support, clear communication, and the consistent message that growth is possible. It's the rock-solid conviction that every student will grow.

Engage. Creating learning that feels real, relevant, and challenging. Work where students see themselves. Where they feel they belong. Where their voices and choices matter. It's igniting the fire that makes them want to learn.

Empower. Gradually releasing control and helping students own their learning. Giving them authority and responsibility. Teaching them to reflect on their own growth. Creating space for them to fail, learn, and try again. It's helping them build the agency needed to become the architects of their own futures.

This book provides the necessary framework. It gives you the research. And more importantly, it gives you the concrete strategies you can implement in your school or classroom tomorrow. Stories of what's worked. Real obstacles and how they were overcome. Practical guidance grounded in both research and decades of educator experience.

What I love most is that Laurie and Patti write with such conviction and humility. They're *not* saying, "Do this, and you'll fix everything." They're saying: "Here's what research shows. Here's what we've seen firsthand. Here's how to build it where you are, with the students you have." That's honest. That's hopeful. *That's what we need right now.*

Because every student who walks into a school building deserves to be *expected* to succeed. Not perfunctorily. Not for a mission statement. But genuinely, deeply believed in by the adults around them. Each student deserves to be *engaged* in work that connects to her life and her questions and feels worth doing. Each student deserves to be *empowered* to direct his own learning, make real choices, and gradually become capable of thinking and acting independently. When we get this right, students don't just do better in school. They become people who believe in themselves.

You have the power to make that happen for those you serve. This book will show you how.

—Thomas C. Murray
　　Director of Innovation for *Future Ready Schools*

Destination: Powerful Learning

*P*ower: *strength; skill; authority; the ability to act; the capability to produce a desired effect or influence; the capacity to do something great; the confidence to achieve control over oneself and some aspects of one's environment*

All these definitions of power describe ideas and hopes educators have for our students. And all are among the most important components integral to the definition of *powerful learning.*

Powerful learning is the intentional, cumulative set of learning plans and experiences that promote development of deep understandings, core competencies, high personal investment and passion in learning, and strong real-world connections needed for students' lives.[1]

The power *lies in students gaining knowledge, meaning, values, and purpose from what they learn. It lies in students becoming equipped with the cognitive, social, and emotional competencies and mindsets necessary to thrive, change, contribute, and make a difference in a complex world. When we say, "becoming equipped," we mean prepared and supplied for today, for every day of their* *future schooling, and for their lives outside of and beyond school. The power of such learning leads to many positive outcomes beyond educational attainment and successful careers, deep into personal and social health and well-being. Powerful learning should be the priority of every school; every student has the right to the benefits of this process.*

Foundations of Powerful Learning

Many school structures and practices support powerful learning. It flourishes best in a safe, inclusive, caring school community and culture of shared values, vision, and understanding about how to put those to work. School communities with the highest success at powerful learning are also filled with passion and positivity in their belief in (and commitment to) the capabilities and growth of all students. Powerful learning is supported by:

- A school community culture of thinking and growth mindset with high value on learning, competence, and well-being for every student.
- Rigorous curricula with context-appropriate content that is challenging, personally relevant, and applicable to diverse topics and real-world contexts, guided by well-qualified educators who provide engaging instruction based on evidence-based practices.
- Foundational learning in literacy, numeracy, and technology with practice in adapting and applying it to new contexts and topics.
- Teaching and modeling a wide range of learning strategies and skills that cross content areas and social and personal situations. These proficiencies include: curiosity, critical thinking, creative thinking, metacognition, decision-making, citizenship,

collaboration, problem solving, exploration, questioning, sharing perspectives and ideas, self-expression, self-understanding and examination, self-management, personal agency, citizenship, resilience, communication, meaningful use of technology, and learning from failure.

- Strong, respectful, caring relationships among all members of the school community with emphasis on contributing to one another and to the wider world.

- Priorities set on high levels of active student voice and involvement in shaping and managing their school lives and personal learning and on strong engagement with students' families.

- Consistent monitoring of the quality of learning (depth of thinking, understanding, and meaningfulness of learning for each student).

The Pathways: A Dynamic Instructional Trio

Our purpose is to offer ways for educators to design learning settings and experiences that cultivate and further powerful learning for all students. In our years as educators, we have worked with thousands of students and educators who have demonstrated practices that meet this goal. We've noticed that many of the best practices for learning fall into three broad instructional approaches that lead to effective results. Each approach contributes to powerful learning. Together, they have a significant impact on how effectively students learn:

Expect! *Instructional approach that designs and communicates high expectations and guides students to reach them with personalized support.*

Engage! *Instructional approach that fuels and sustains students' deep investment in their learning.*

Empower! *Instructional approach that ignites and strengthens students' autonomy and agency, enabling them to take ownership of their learning and personal growth.*

We describe these approaches as **pathways to powerful learning**, because we see this happening:

1. With actions and experiences from these three approaches, students (accompanied by their teachers and other school staff and supported by their families) make forward progress, moving along thoughtfully-planned routes that offer sensible sequence–increasing challenge and cumulative understanding as students pursue goals. The pathways include "mile-markers" of accomplishment along the way and destinations that are clear, although sometimes new discoveries along the way alter the destination somewhat.

2. More than just metaphors, the pathways are concrete experiences for students. Each student is on an actual personal journey–a unique and valuable ongoing experience. As students travel, they develop and mature, gaining mindsets, knowledge, confidence, and skills to gradually become independent learners heavily involved in directing their own learning pathways. They encounter and navigate real obstacles and challenges along the way. Their routes bring them into connection with other learners and mentors; they grow in their abilities to cooperate and learn in collaboration.

3. In addition to our own experiences affirming the forceful effects of these three instructional approaches, we have found that the actions are well-researched and proven effective in leading to powerful learning.

All three pathways begin with belief, require specific actions to develop skills that students need, and use particular supports to reach goals. None of these are pathways that end; students keep moving, learning, and discovering for a lifetime. Although we'll address each pathway separately, these routes to powerful learning are, indeed, inseparable and often occur simultaneously. They run on the same "concourse," overlapping and intertwining. You'll read similar themes and practices in each of the book's three parts. This repetition is intentional, because actions and strategies described within any pathway or chapter support growth in and draw strength from one another.

Picture students accompanied on these pathways by parents or caregivers and then by different teachers over the years, with others at school joining along at various times. As a teacher, value the precious time that you have to walk beside each of your students on their journeys. And do your best to facilitate the most powerful learning you can while you have that privilege and responsibility.

What's in This Book?

The book has three parts, one for each pathway of actions (Expect! Engage! Empower!). Each of the parts has an introductory section that addresses the first two questions below and five chapters that address the third.

What? *Definitions and broader meanings of the pathway*

Why? *Research-backed benefits and reasons why this instructional approach drives powerful learning*

How? *Descriptions of best actions that lead to powerful learning experiences for students*

Chapters: *Within each of the three book parts (the pathways), every chapter focuses on a key instructional goal that contributes to progress along that pathway. The chapter describes concrete actions (with practical strategies, practices, and examples that work to accomplish the actions) proven to help educators guide students toward meeting the goal.*

Stories: *The goals, actions, and strategies presented in each chapter are interspersed with real-life stories and anecdotes. These offer deeply personal, compelling examples of the journey toward the chapter's powerful learning goal as experienced and remembered by actual students, teachers, or leaders, including from us (Laurie and Patti) and some of our colleagues.*

References: Citations and references are indicated with numbers; these connect to a full description of each resource and can be found at the end of the book in the "Endnotes" section.

Who's the Audience?

Information, concepts, and strategies in this book will be useful to:

- Teachers at all grade levels, subject areas, and levels of experience
- School leaders
- Paraprofessionals
- Instructional and learning coaches
- Curriculum specialists
- Other school staff members
- Pre-service teachers
- Tutors

- Homeschoolers
- Parents and caregivers

How Can This Book Be Used?

Each of the three parts addresses one instructional pathway. We recommend that you approach each with a thorough reading of the introductory section to that part. This will set the context and background understanding for the chapters and strategies that follow.

Just as audiences are broad, so are settings and times when this information can be used. Think about reading, discussing, or using practices when a teacher is working alone or with others to broaden skills in supporting powerful learning. For example:

- Educators planning together in staff, team, department, or grade-level meetings
- Teachers learning together in professional development sessions
- Leaders learning together
- Mentors working with mentees
- Parents, caregivers, or tutors teaching and learning in home-school settings

The strategies are easy to read and ready to use. Any one can readily be adapted to your specific students, content area, or setting. You might practice the suggestions in one part of the book at a time, one strategy (chapter) at a time, or one of the actions within a chapter at a time.

Some instructional strategies for powerful learning may be new to you. Find support from colleagues, and work on your teaching skills together. Share your experiences, challenges, and successes with designing and promoting powerful learning. When you support each other, you'll grow faster–and so will your students.

PART I

Expect!

Introduction

WHAT?
A Picture of Expectations

Every school is filled with expectations. Each day, teachers, leaders, students, and families hold expectations of one another, and because these expectations are interconnected, they all inevitably shape students' experiences and outcomes.

However, when we examine and describe EXPECT as a pathway to powerful learning, it is **teachers' expectations for students** that have the most profound influence. This influence extends to academic performance and accomplishments, behavior, effort, work patterns, accountability, competence, attitude, communication, social interactions, and—of utmost importance—to students' self-expectations and self-belief.

Because of their strength, teacher expectations are emphasized in this part of the book. Yet expectations from others in the school community can have similar effects on students. **Thus, all the influences and messages that we offer about expectations are applicable to others who are part of our students' lives** (influences from parents and caregivers, non-teaching staff, school leaders, coaches, volunteers, and peers).

Definitions

Expectations for students: beliefs about and in students, about the potential they have to achieve; about their probable behaviors, characteristics, or accomplishments now and in the future.

High teacher expectations for all students: a teacher's belief that all students are capable of achieving or performing well and that, regardless of their challenges or backgrounds, all students can and will (with the right support) move beyond their current level of performance, working hard toward their potential.

More about the Meaning of High Expectations

There is plenty of rhetoric from educators and researchers surrounding the concept of high expectations. Surprisingly, few define what that actually means. It is not always clear (especially to students or families and sometimes to teachers) exactly what a high expectation is. What does it look like when someone strives for or meets high expectations? The answer is far more complex than getting top scores on tests or high grades on report cards.

High expectations are those that go beyond the basic requirements and beyond a student's individual achievement. Such expectations challenge students to reach above their usual level of accomplishment. They require commitment, in-depth study, critical thinking, complex analysis and understanding, and broad applications of material or principles. **Here's what efforts toward high expectations look like in the school and classroom:**

Teachers believe that the capacity for competence lies within each student; they vigorously advocate and work for the needs of each student, focusing their efforts to develop students' strengths to help each one succeed. They hold a commitment to excellence and provide challenging content and tasks for all students. They consistently (and visibly) model and reinforce high expectations.

Students push to exceed beyond the minimum, continuously digging deeper to learn and understand more. They do their work well, not just enough to get finished or pass the class but, instead, consistently and thoroughly completing assignments and homework. They take on the challenge of difficult tasks in order to meet their goals. They show strong connections to their learning and are able to demonstrate, explain, interpret, and apply concepts and skills they've learned. They express belief in themselves as capable of meeting high expectations.

Myths about High Expectations

There is no doubt that high expectations are a foundation of a school culture that helps students thrive. Yet, some assumptions about high expectations are only partially true or are completely false.

Myth: Not all students are capable of meeting high expectations.

Most educators say high expectations are absolutely necessary to quality learning. And most educators would say they believe all students can reach high expectations. Yet, consciously or not, teacher beliefs about some students may be swayed by student characteristics. Thus, some teachers do hold unjustifiably low expectations for achievement (or behavior) of a student or group of students based on such characteristics as poor behavior, gender, race, socioeconomic status, and a host of other personal, family, or societal factors that have nothing to do with the actual academic potential of a student.

Myth: If we want all students to reach high expectations, we'll have to lower expectations some.

Believing all students will grow and succeed with rigorous expectations does not mean that you must adjust or lower your expectations so all students can reach them. Classes consist of students with a variety of capabilities. Not all students will excel at (or even study) calculus, take an AP course, write an award-winning essay, or attend and graduate from college. Therefore, recognize that each student will not pursue **the same** high expectations and outcomes; and not everyone will meet the same academic or non-academic goals in exactly the same way at the same time.

Remember, however, that the powerful **"reach-high" mindset** at the very core of education—the mindset that relentlessly encourages all students to push toward their potential success—**IS the same for everyone.** The common expectation is that **all** can and will reach **their** full potential. Consider: We don't lower expectations. We don't differentiate the quality of instruction as in making something less or more quality in nature. Nothing is diminished for some students; everything is high-quality instruction. We do adjust the support during the learning, however, depending upon what students need. We personalize support, remove barriers to success, and design a pathway that helps each individual student succeed.

Myth: When teachers (or school mission statements) simply articulate a belief that all students are capable of reaching high standards, students understand and believe this.

Researchers find a gap (sometimes quite wide) between what teachers think they communicate and what students actually perceive.

Students may hear the words telling them that teachers believe in them but may not necessarily get this message. Students may hear the statement of an expectation but may not fully understand what's being said or have any idea how to reach the expectation. Here's the thing: students are not only listening to what is said; they are also "listening" to a host of implicit nonverbal communications and actions that convey teachers' beliefs. These messages come through adults' gestures, facial expressions, attitudes, accessibility, type of support (or lack thereof), the way the adult disciplines or evaluates them, or a teacher's (or leader's) treatment of them in comparison to other students.

Myth: Setting high expectations or creating a rigorous curriculum embedded with high expectations will lead to higher levels of student performance and achievement.

Educators get used to these assumptions. In the promotion of high standards, we repeatedly hear about "setting school-wide high expectations" and "holding students accountable for reaching high expectations." Too often, the talk about expectations implies that it is mostly the job of students to rise to the challenges, dive into the rigor, and reach high. Such an approach of "setting and expecting students to meet" (no matter how thoughtfully expectations are crafted or how excellent the curriculum) is not enough. It must be accompanied by school processes and teacher behaviors that visibly prove stated beliefs and masterfully support every student along the entire pathway to reaching high expectations. Educators must meet high expectations for their assistance to students. Students can't succeed unless we do our part.

WHY?
The Power of Expectations

Teacher expectations can create barriers or inspire students to leap barriers. We've learned from years of research and concrete experience that students' success tends to rise or fall in direct relation to the expectations placed upon them.

Most educators know about the 1964 Rosenthal and Jacobson study on teacher expectations that led to their description of "the Pygmalion Effect." The researchers gave teachers a list of students in each class who they said had been identified (by an IQ test) as likely to make substantial academic gains that year. Twenty percent of the total number of students in each class were randomly (and falsely) identified. When those students were retested later in the year, students in the experimental group (labeled as having higher IQs) showed significantly greater gains in IQ scores when compared to the control group. Researchers concluded that teachers treated those students differently because of the expectation that they would flourish, thus contributing to the increase.[1] This study has become a cornerstone of educational viewpoints on teacher expectations. The findings have been re-affirmed in hundreds of further studies.[2] Its message has been put into practice to varying degrees.

> Teacher expectations can create barriers or inspire students to leap barriers.

Some Discoveries about Teacher Expectations

Countless research studies reveal the power of teacher expectations. Here are some general findings:[3]

1. Teacher expectations and teacher estimates of achievement for students are among the highest of all influences on student learning and achievement. Students tend to live up or down to teacher expectations (whether they are high, low, or in between).

2. Students pick up on teachers' expectations, even if teachers themselves are not aware of them. Expectations are communicated by inferences, verbal and nonverbal, even when teachers are not conscious of the expectation or of their behavior. Students notice and compare perceived teacher expectations of themselves and other students.

3. What a teacher believes about a student's potential for success may lead the teacher (often unconsciously) to differentiate teaching behavior in line with general senses about how the student will achieve or behave. These beliefs become the cornerstone to all the teacher's expectations and instructional choices for a class or individual. Students perceive differentiated teacher behaviors.

4. Students readily internalize the teacher's expectations, thus raising or lowering their self-expectations, changing their belief in themselves, and adapting their behaviors to match what they think the teacher believes. Because of this, a given student's beliefs about individual capabilities can be different in different classes based on the different expectations of different teachers.

5. Teachers' expectations set the tone for expectations students have of their peers as well.

6. Effects of teacher expectations accumulate over time, and the influence grows significantly throughout the years students spend in school.

7. Teacher expectations are highly predictive of students' future educational attainment.

Benefits of High Teacher Expectations

All the powers and benefits of high expectations described below **only result** when they are set and expected in a context where:

1. The teacher and other educators hold, and clearly demonstrate with their behavior, the rock-solid belief in the capability of all students to meet high expectations.
2. High expectations are reachable, appropriate, relevant, fitted to individual students, communicated and explained clearly, and actually understood by students.
3. Individual students' efforts toward high expectations are encouraged with the specific guidance and support needed to reach the expectations.
4. Efforts (not just final outcomes) are consistently affirmed, and progress is regularly celebrated.

Whenever we discuss the concept of *high expectations* for all students, understand that we include the above four conditions as part of the terminology. Here are some positive outcomes that result from high expectations pursued in such a context:[4]

- When teachers expect that certain students **will** show greater intellectual or academic growth, students believe it, and they **do** show such growth.
- When teachers expect students to go on to graduate from college, they are more likely to do so.
- Teachers' high expectations of a student raise the perspective peers have of that student. And when peers have high expectations of one another, they all tend to do better.
- Teachers who overestimate the ability of students get better results in student academic growth than teachers who underestimate the ability.

- When students experience progress toward and attainment of high expectations, they are likely to:
    - Engage more deeply with what they are learning and with other learners.
    - Be willing to challenge themselves.
    - Gain confidence and pride in their academic and personal growth.
    - Improve behavior, self-management, and work habits.
    - Show increased self-belief, enthusiasm, motivation, and interest.
    - Have better attendance and lower dropout rates.
    - Show more persistence and greater resilience.
    - Take ownership of their own behavior and learning.
    - Experience joy and hope in their academic and personal accomplishments.

Consequences of Low Teacher Expectations

Although teachers rarely hold low expectations for individuals or groups of students intentionally, many do subconsciously, and they have unwittingly communicated low expectations for some of their students. It is critical to raise awareness of low expectations, because the effects can be devastating:[5]

- When the teacher **does not believe** that certain students are capable of performing at high levels in their class or subject, those students generally **don't**.
- When teachers expect students **not** to go on to graduate from college, they are more likely **not** to do so.
- When students sense a teacher's low expectations for them, they internalize low expectations for themselves. When students perceive a teacher's doubts about them, this confirms students'

worst fears about their own potential. And just as troubling, peers often adopt the teacher's low expectations of that student or group of students.

+ Teachers who underestimate the ability of students get lower academic results than teachers who overestimate students' abilities.

+ Teachers' communication of low expectations has more power to limit student achievement than communication of high expectations has to raise student performance.

+ Students who perceive that a teacher has low expectations for them often

  + Stop caring about school or pretend not to care.

  + Show increased frustration, discouragement, or withdrawal.

  + Lose confidence, perceive themselves as incompetent, or have self-disparaging thoughts.

  + Don't trust in (or continue to sustain) successes they do have.

  + Have less perseverance and resilience in their work.

  + Are reluctant to try, take risks, or embrace new challenges.

  + Feel that their academic abilities are undervalued.

HOW?
The Pathway to High Expectations

Given the broad effects of teacher expectations on students' own expectations, self-belief, performance, and future educational trajectories, how do educators make good use of this power to help students reach for and attain high expectations?

The desire to increase student understanding and attainment of high standards draws us logically to consider a teacher's enthusiasm for the journey, safe classrooms where everyone is seen as capable of meeting high expectations and where everyone benefits from equitable resources, and learning activities along with excellent instruction and personalized support. In such a context, we can take intentional actions proven to lead to success with high expectations. In Part 1 of this book, we explore these elements of expectations more through **clear and worthwhile expectations, high-quality teacher support, high academic aims, success with grade-level instruction,** and **meaningful feedback**. Each of the following chapters (1-5) describes a specific, concrete action with supporting strategies to spark, nurture, and sustain engagement. The recommended behaviors and practices are observable to our students, ourselves, and others. They can be intentionally practiced, honed, and, in many cases, measured.

Although Part 1 focuses on expectations, you'll find that, as students hone the attitudes and practices of striving for high expectations (and the satisfaction of reaching them), their **engagement** (investment in learning) and **empowerment** grow by leaps and bounds.

CHAPTER 1

EXPECT Students to Strive for Clear and Worthwhile Expectations

When I (Patti) was about eleven years old, my mom and I traveled to Arkansas to visit family. One morning at my grandparents' farm, I asked if I could walk to Uncle Beryl's farm because he had lots of animals—especially horses! He lived about a mile down the road, and while I assured my mom I could make the walk, I did ask her to remind me which road to take at the fork.

She told me to remember: "Do not go past the old schoolhouse." Confident that I understood, I set out expecting to arrive safely at Uncle Beryl's. My mom was equally sure I knew the way.

When I came to the fork, I took the road to the left so that I did not go past the schoolhouse. Long story short, I became seriously lost on the backroads of rural Arkansas. What my mom meant was not to take the road that goes past (in front of) the schoolhouse. What I heard was not to go past (no further than) the schoolhouse itself. That small misunderstanding turned into quite an adventure and a memorable lifelong lesson about the importance of clear communication.

When we set expectations that are not meaningful or, as above, are poorly communicated, we invite chaos and confusion; we sabotage our goals of setting high standards and helping students reach them. To avoid this, we must commit to consistently setting expectations appropriate for students' capabilities and personal and academic needs. We must also assure that our expectations for academic accomplishments and classroom conduct are crystal clear to students. Well-conceived, well-suited, and purposeful expectations that are understood by students offer:

+ Inspiration and engagement that energizes students.
+ Stability, consistency, and clarity in knowing where they are headed and what they are supposed to do.
+ Support for students' self-direction and self-regulation as they navigate their learning tasks and personal behavior.
+ Positive classroom management, as students waste less time and have less confusion when they know and understand the expectations (which promotes smoother transitions and a more productive classroom environment).

Put It Into Practice

Know What You Expect and Why

The right expectations, well-communicated, have a positive influence on student learning. These begin with your own clarity about what students need and what you expect.

+ Reflect on and analyze your expectations. Ask yourself:
  Am I asking students to do something that is new to them?
  How simple or complex is the task I am asking students to complete?
  How many different tasks are involved in completing the assignment?

Will they have the knowledge and capabilities to complete the assignment on their own, or will they need additional help and support? Have I built a student's learning capacity for the learning to come? If not, what can I do to build that capacity?

+ Identify your purposes, goals, and success criteria for academic and nonacademic procedures and for each learning expectation. Make sure students know and understand them. When students don't follow directions, it could be that they weren't listening. It could also be that your directions were not clear. Or perhaps a student (or more than one) didn't understand the goal. Read and follow the suggestions in the upcoming section in this chapter, "Communicate expectations clearly." Connect with any student who still doesn't understand to find out why and decide what approach is needed to help.

+ Make sure you haven't confused students with extra expectations unrelated to the main goal. If the learning target is to convert statistical information (from any subject) into a line graph, don't expect them to write a summary of the information unless that is also a separate, well-explained goal.

Establish Consistent Protocols and Routines

The overall culture of the classroom plays a vital role in high expectations. We want students to develop a strong work ethic and confidence in their capabilities. This can only be done in an environment that values academic excellence, hard work, and the possibility of great progress. Consistency of practices provides and sustains a safe and productive climate, positive behavior, and belonging.

> The overall culture of the classroom plays a vital role in high expectations.

When students know what to expect on a daily basis, it is easier for them to follow expected routines and behaviors.

- Determine which protocols are most critical to your class. Choose those that are needed for the practices or situations that are in your upcoming plans. Recall protocols that you needed in this class or grade level last year–routines that would have been helpful to establish. Maybe it's an opening routine, how to hand in assignments, ways to ask for help, fire drill procedures, or how to organize and manage materials. (Who knew that asking to sharpen a pencil could derail an entire class?)
- Introduce protocols one (or a few) at time, when they are needed. Don't waste students' time teaching procedures for all-school assemblies weeks before the first assembly.
- Avoid "telling" students about routines and protocols. Instead, show them (often). Project a sample of proper heading on papers. Demonstrate earbud use or a dress code violation. Invite a colleague to join you in holding a "mock" student-led parent conference (done correctly and incorrectly). Look at this as part of your curriculum, and use teaching strategies with time for students to practice.

Involve Students in Setting Expectations

When students have a role in creating expectations, they are more likely to embrace, remember, and work to reach them.[1] Trust students to take part in designing, describing, and demonstrating expectations for learning and working together for academic behavior and progress. When appropriate, invite them to join in decisions about what is needed, how to explain expectations clearly, and how to follow them consistently. Let students help develop a scoring guide for an assignment, determine some basic class rules (kids, as well as teachers, hate it when their peers are yelling at others in class), or establish individual classroom roles. Or ask something like this: *What will help us end class without chaos but also help everyone end feeling good about class?* Tackle one routine or procedure at a time. For expectations you have set or suggested, include students in demonstrating them. With established routines, include students in reflections on how they are working and what revisions might be needed.

Create Worthwhile Expectations

An expectation is of little use to students or teachers if it is superficial or simply feels like pleasing the teacher, which we must remember when we set expectations to further students' development as good citizens in the classroom or their growth in deep thinking and other aspects of powerful learning. Expectations for students must be:

- **Meaningful:** Show clear significance and purpose and are valid skills and topics that have applications relevant and useful to individual students in their classes or other parts of their lives.
- **Rigorous:** Provide students with cognitive challenge that stretches them while remaining attainable.
- **Achievable:** Ensure the expectation can be met with the available time, resources, and skill level. Align expectations with students' readiness, maturity, and available support.
- **Observable and measurable:** Require behaviors or outcomes that allow progress to be monitored.
- **Time-based:** Let students know how much time they have. If a time restriction or deadline is needed for all or parts of an assignment, these must be clear ahead of time.

Here are some examples of expectations that are purposeful in contrast to those that are not:

One kindergarten teacher shares this rule with students: *Respect each other's personal space and belongings.* The teacher down the hall says (and demonstrates, using a hula hoop): *Keep your hands off others. Pretend all kids in this room have a hula hoop around their body at all times. Stay outside of that hula hoop. This will show that you respect their personal space. And do not touch each other's backpacks, clothing, or other belongings.*

A 6th-grade science teacher gives an assignment to create a diagram, drawing, or model that shows the water cycle. The science teacher across the hall assigns students the task of depicting the water cycle in a way that explains (without you telling them) to any viewer of their grade-level or older what a water cycle is, how it works, why it matters and includes a definition of Earth's atmosphere system and an explanation of the processes of evaporation, transpiration, condensation, precipitation, and runoff.

Communicate Expectations Clearly

As a school administrator, I (Laurie) have visited thousands of classes over the years. When I see a class where things aren't going well and a teacher is frustrated, a discussion often reveals that their frustration can be traced back to lack of teacher clarity. Seeing a teacher reflect on this realization can be very powerful. We give directions that we've given over direct objects in English or fractions in math (ones we give year after year after year). Sometimes, we forget that this is the first time students are hearing these directions, and we unintentionally leave out key aspects. Providing clear, specific steps to expectations and asking students to repeat them to show understanding helps prevent confusion, builds trust, and ensures that everyone understands expectations. In order to ensure clarity:

- Be clear in your mind about exactly what is expected of students. Teachers' clarity about their own intentions combined with clarity to students has a powerful, positive effect on student learning.[2] Take the critical step of breaking down a learning target or standard into its specific elements (look for the verbs). Collaborate with colleagues who teach your same subject. To be sure of our expectations for a learning experience, we must clarify each step of the process for ourselves.

- Be explicit and concise. Students must understand just what to do. No matter students' ages, show what it looks like to meet the expectation. Again, telling alone is not effective. Provide models and examples. Give and discuss rubrics (matrices that have ratings and descriptions of levels of performance in relation to a desired outcome for a learning task) Provide time and guidelines for students to apply the criteria of the rubric to analyze samples of the intended product, helping students understand the criteria and be able to apply them to their own product as they work.

- Ensure that students know precise meanings of specific words or phrases within an expectation. Define such things as: *clear, creative, complete, polish, cite evidence, on time, participate, outline, diagram, proof,* or *main ideas.* Tailor the definition to the assignment at hand. Show or create in front of them a sample of an outline for a similar product. Add to their agendas the times and dates for this being *on time.* Provide an example of a product that is *complete* as opposed to one that is not. Guide a mini-lesson in *citing evidence,* using a similar product as your assignment. After describing a requirement or task, ask students to describe or demonstrate what it would mean to participate fully.

- Help students understand not just **what** is expected, but also **why** and **how.** Telling them something must be learned because it's "a state standard" or "on the test" rarely motivates. For example, after studying the Colonial period, tell students they'll create a timeline showing key events leading to the Revolution using information from their class resources (the ***what***). Show sample timelines with different formats, then discuss the components of a timeline and how information is organized and labeled. This helps students see how to complete their own. Next, show a timeline of discoveries leading to the smartphones they use today and discuss **why** timelines are useful. It helps them visualize sequences, see patterns, understand causes and effects, and recognize how events connect. They can then discuss how specific events contributed to or interacted with the others.

+ Break down complex expectations. Each student (even the most talented or capable) has a limit to how much cognitive load can be handled at a time. And, as the number or complexity of directions increases, it becomes more challenging for students to process those directions, especially for younger students (whose working memory is not as strong as older students) as well as for students with learning differences, language barriers, or attention difficulties. Identify specific actions needed to complete that step. Provide lists, charts, diagrams, or other visual representations of the steps. Completing each part is satisfying for students, builds confidence, and keeps them engaged (and makes the task more do-able).

+ Do quick formative assessments at each step, making the expectation more attainable, ensuring understanding before the student moves on, and providing success with each step. Give any support needed for the student to confidently complete a step. Conquering one smaller portion of the task reduces frustrations and mistakes. It also promotes independence and enables students greater access to reaching high expectations.

In my (Laurie's) second year teaching 10th-grade English, we read several short stories. For each story, students completed a chart on its literary devices. The unit ended with a comprehensive poster project showing what they'd learned about the literary building blocks of short stories. I made a quick rubric to go with it (no ChatGPT back then!), mostly to make grading easier. Though I handed it out and went over it, I (apparently) didn't take time to ensure students understood it or to gather their feedback on its clarity or usefulness.

The projects were due right before winter break, and semester grades were due shortly after, so I was determined to get them quickly graded before heading home for winter break. Sitting on the floor of my classroom, surrounded by fifty poster boards, I quickly realized my rubric was a disaster; it was vague, rushed, and unclear. Poster board after poster board, I grew more and more frustrated. How had they even used it to complete the project? No wonder the projects didn't match my expectations. The expectations in my mind had not made it to the poster boards, and I was very frustrated with students for poor quality work after weeks spent on this unit. By about the twentieth poster, it hit me: the problem wasn't students' effort, but my poor guidance. I scrapped the generic rubric (where I was looking for very specific details within overly broad criteria such as "includes literary elements" and "demonstrates understanding of story") and started grading again (using my best judgement of an overall product—not exactly best practice for assessment of student knowledge). It was certainly fairer to them, if not to my workload.

The next year, I spent far more time crafting and discussing the rubric before starting the project (with much clearer expectation criteria such as "clearly explains how multiple literary elements such as characterization, conflict, and symbolism develop the theme of each story" and "cites specific textual evidence to explain the theme of the story"). That investment paid off, and the project became a favorite and a truly effective measure of students' understanding of literary devices.

EXPECT Students to Receive High-Quality Teacher Support

A team of language arts teachers at Patti's middle school were concerned about some students who were consistently struggling with the content and thus falling further and further behind. They brainstormed together and came up with a plan to develop a "morning academy" to meet two days a week. Struggling students came to school about twenty minutes early to attend a short, fifteen-minute introductory lesson. Instead of remediating the selected students, teachers pre-taught them the content so that when they were exposed to it during the regular class period they were already familiar with the concepts.

What happened next was amazing. Because these students had been exposed to the concept ahead of time, when the lesson was taught to the entire class the students started participating and answering questions instead of being confused and off task. The personalized approach to their instruction helped these students meet the standards. Plus, it gave a boost to their self-esteem and confidence, making a positive difference in their attitudes and behavior.

As we've emphasized earlier, holding high expectations for students (even when the expectations are expertly crafted and well communicated) is not enough. In order for them to actually succeed, we must provide intentional, high-quality support for students in their efforts to reach academic expectations and success. All students should expect teaching attitudes and practices that provide this kind of success. In essence, personalized support within a classroom of high expectations means combining belief in every learner's potential with intentional, flexible, and student-centered teaching to ensure **every student can achieve meaningful growth and success.**

Todd Whitaker, author of *What Great Teachers Do Differently* identifies this as one of 17 things teachers do that matter most: "Great teachers have high expectations for students but even higher expectations for themselves."[1] Student success depends heavily on the quality and consistency of teacher support, so don't expect more from students than you are willing to demand of yourself. Your commitment to setting and supporting high standards in instruction and behavior will directly shape your students' achievement. Students are always watching (and often imitate what they see).

> Student success depends heavily on the quality and consistency of teacher support, so don't expect more from students than you are willing to demand of yourself.

Put It Into Practice

Believe in Every Student

Teacher belief in every student is a powerful support for helping students believe in themselves and reach high expectations. But your belief, alone, is not enough. It is only powerful when students are **convinced** that you actually believe in them. The sincerity of your belief is revealed by the way you communicate expectations and the behaviors and treatment students experience.[2] In a study of how teacher expectations affect student belief, researchers Olivia Johnston, Helen Wildly, and Jennifer Shand found that their results concur with other self-efficacy research: "Students' beliefs about themselves as learners are shaped by the teacher's communication of expectations for students, so that when the teacher conveys a belief that the student can succeed at school, the student believes it too and acts accordingly."[3]

- Demonstrate your genuine belief in every student:
    - Treat students as if you expect them to do the right thing, recognizing their positive actions and choices.
    - Acknowledge students' skills, accomplishments, strengths, and growth.
    - Get to know students as individuals by learning about their interests, backgrounds, needs, and hopes. Build daily connections. Interact with each student every day (even if only a brief private check-in or positive comment on their work or behavior).
    - Write notes of affirmation for specific accomplishments or progress.
    - Promote positive peer relationships through collaboration and teamwork.
    - Respect students' dignity and privacy by addressing concerns individually and fairly.
    - Avoid whole-class consequences for individual student behavior. (It's rare that every single student is guilty of the behavior in question.)
    - Allow do-overs (for full credit) to support learning, growth, and improvement.

- Trust students with responsibility for their learning and the classroom community.
- Be credible. *Credibility* is the quality of being believable and trustworthy. Teacher credibility has a strong, positive influence on student learning.[4] To be credible, make sure students see that you treat everyone fairly and that you are approachable and caring to all. Tell them that no one is alone and that they can rely on you to be available, interested, and helpful. Then, **be** those things. Follow through on what you promise you will do. Demonstrate your enthusiasm about your job and that you are glad each one is your student. Honor them by knowing your content well and by being organized and confident in your teaching. A teacher who is poorly prepared, has haphazard instruction, or appears unable to help students understand the content will be less credible to students.
- Show belief through what you say (and don't say). Remember that students are highly attuned to everything you say and do. Even when they appear to be unaware or disinterested, they notice differences in teachers' communications from class to class or student to student. When students perceive inconsistent expectations and behavior from student to student or class to class, the teacher loses credibility. Individual students pick up messages that they are "less worthy (capable, likeable) than" or "better than" other students.
  - Tell students often, *I believe in you.*
  - Express belief in their ability to grow, improve, and reach goals. Point out and celebrate progress, even the small steps.
  - Make sure your tone, facial expressions, gestures, and energy match your words. You might say, *That's a great solution.* But if your voice is monotone and conveys no passion or your face shows no joy, the student won't believe that you really think it's great.

- Pay attention to how students respond to your communication. If a student's face falls or scowls, if she pulls away, or if he looks deflated, you'll know that you have not conveyed belief.
- Be aware of your words or gestures that may show doubt, approval, or disapproval. The tone and excitement (or lack thereof) in your voice or gestures of turning away, stepping back, crossing your arms, being tense, or being relaxed and enthusiastic tells students a lot.
- Ensure that all students (even challenging ones) receive praise, support, and recognition for effort and progress.
- Help students believe in themselves. Student *self-efficacy* (belief in one's own ability to succeed at a particular task or goal or group of tasks or goals) has a high impact on student learning.[5] It is a major foundation for students' internalization and pursuit of high standards. Here are some ways to help students increase self-efficacy:
  - Teach students the difference between a *growth mindset* and *fixed mindset* and help them identify areas where they can continue to grow and learn. A *mindset* is a state of mind, a way of thinking, or a set of beliefs and attitudes that influences how one sees oneself and the world.[6] According to Carol Dweck, Stanford University professor and leading expert on mindset, "In a fixed mindset, people believe their basic qualities, like their intelligence or talent, are simply fixed traits. Alternatively, in a growth mindset, people believe that their most basic abilities can be developed through dedication and hard work—brains and talent are just the starting point. . . that they can become smarter if they work hard and persevere—may learn more and view challenges and failures as opportunities to improve and grow."[7] (See more about growth mindset in Chapter 13.)

- Promote and affirm effort, progress, and improvement over ability. Use the power of "yet" to reinforce learning over time. This is a mark of a growth-mindset alternative to failure or fear of failure. Instead of giving up on something before you start or after you're started but have hit a wall, you believe that you can still find a path to success. Teach this to students and help them find tools and new approaches to get moving toward a goal, all propelled by the "not-yet" attitude.
- Acknowledge that struggles, mistakes, and failures are okay and lead to learning and developing new skills. Share your own learning struggles and how you overcame them.
- Challenge "*I'm not good at this*" thinking by encouraging more positive thoughts and language. Help students rephrase to something like: *I'm having a hard time with this right now, but I can get better with practice.* Or, *I'm going to try a different approach.* Or, *I'll break this down into small steps, and then I can do this.* To overcome negative thoughts and shift to a positive mindset, students can make positive statements that are true of themselves: *I've conquered hard problems before. I am brave enough to try new things.* Also, make time for students to recognize and describe their successes, both small and large. They can write or speak these and share them with each other. Experiences of mastery deepen self-efficacy.
- Frequently share your messages with students and families about their effort, attitude, and growth. The teacher's affirmation of this is a powerful way to put success on display and further boost self-belief. Each month in Laurie's school district, teachers write two positive postcards directly to students and mail them home. Even years later, I still run into students or their family members who tell me their postcard is still proudly displayed on their refrigerator.

Practice High Expectation Teaching

We noted earlier that teacher beliefs about students inevitably affect the way they treat and teach students. Christine Rubie-Davies is a world leader on high expectation teachers and teaching. Following in the steps of research showing that when teachers believe that all students can make large gains and thus all should be treated similarly, she set out to determine how those beliefs teachers translated into teacher actions made the difference for students' progress. Along with fellow researchers, she has identified practices and behaviors characteristic of high expectation teachers. Students who did not get the benefits of such behaviors made little or no academic gains in these studies.[8]

When teachers work with **students for whom they have high expectations (as opposed to students for whom they have lower expectations)**, they are more likely to demonstrate these behaviors and do so more often:

- Manage behavior more positively and create a warm classroom climate.
- Use flexible forms of grouping for instruction (as opposed to ability grouping).
- Teach mastery goal-setting to enhance student motivation and self-belief.
- Provide a framework for learning more often (such factors as purpose, objectives, steps for working, desired outcomes, understanding of how learning will be evaluated, and support during the process).
- Dedicate more time to answering student questions and explaining concepts or processes and supply more feedback (with more of it being positive and substantive).

- Criticize students' work, questions, or responses less often, praise more frequently, and show positive bias when evaluating students' work.
- Offer students more response opportunities and more time for response.
- Supply students with higher-level and more challenging content and instruction, more higher-order thinking questions, and a wider variety and higher level of resources.
- Interact more often and in more supportive, caring ways and give more attention to fostering engagement.
- Offer more choice and autonomy.

Scaffold Strategically

Scaffolding is an essential but temporary support that helps students meet high expectations by guiding them through tasks or concepts they cannot yet complete or understand on their own. The process helps students understand a concept, master a skill or process, or complete challenging tasks with the security of some support. Early scaffolding may simplify tasks to help students succeed, but the goal is to increase challenge and promote higher-level thinking and independence. A final goal is to gradually reduce support as students improve to increase ownership of their learning and enable them to complete the task on their own. As you plan to scaffold learning for students:

- For any content unit, topic, or process, prepare a wide range of techniques and tools that can be adapted to individual students and tasks. Methods may include modeling a task for students as you think aloud to explain what you are doing; giving short, focused mini-lessons to pre-teach key vocabulary, skills, or processes; guiding student practice on a skill; providing visual aids or manipulatives to make abstract ideas concrete; breaking complex tasks into smaller, manageable segments; having peers work together on a task; or offering "stepping stone" questions that increase in complexity. Valuable visual tools, available to students while they work, help students remember, review, and clarify key ideas, concepts, or steps for a process (anchor charts); give them ways to organize and structure learning material (graphic organizers or template of an outline to fill in); and provide concrete structures for planning components, sub-tasks, and a timeline for an assignment (work plans). Assessment tools such as rubrics not only serve for final evaluation but are also useful during their work process to remind students of the qualities and components necessary to reach their goal.

- State a clear strategy. The process of effective scaffolding goes beyond gathering good tools and techniques. To scaffold strategically, you must have a careful and thoughtful plan of action to achieve a specific goal. A scaffold is not just one action you take to help the student manage a difficult task. The full plan of action that moves to independence IS the scaffold. You can use a work plan or graphic organizer to plot the strategy before working with the student. Share this plan with the student, allowing time for questions before and during the process. As part of the plan:

  - Clarify the topic, skill, concept, and process for which a student (or group of students) needs support; state a specific intended goal or outcome. This involves identifying what the student presently knows and can do as well as the end goal.

  - Determine how the learning will progress, outlining steps or milestones that build from where the student starts to where the student needs to be. Decide what tools to offer for each part of the learning process.

- Plan where, when, and how you'll make assessments and give feedback to students (exit tickets, brief conferences, check-ins) and how you'll use the assessment information to adjust actions for next steps.
- Decide how and when to scale back support along the way, and set your criteria for the point at which full responsibility for the task will be turned over to the student.

For example: With some third-graders having difficulty finding meaning in poems, the teacher scaffolds this way: She reads aloud the first verse of the poem "Your World" by Georgia Douglas Johnson. Next, she projects or gives a copy of the first four lines and helps students define any words (using context) they may not know (*abide*). She continues with these comments and questions, circling words and phrases and writing down their ideas as they answer. *Who is the speaker in this poem? Who is the speaker addressing? How can you tell? What words or phrases help you visualize what the speaker is describing?* (At this point, students have a few minutes to do quick drawings of what they "see.") *What point is the speaker making in the first verse? Why do you think this?* With this first verse, the teacher models (adds) her own thinking to push students toward deeper thinking.

She shows and reads the next four lines, giving similar prompts and questions but with students jotting or sharing their responses. The teacher adds questions or comments to their responses as needed to push for deeper understanding. With the final four lines, she helps students clarify word meanings, then leaves them with some written prompts, and students finish the poem analysis on their own. They share ideas about the main message of the entire poem. A teacher colleague shared this story with us:

It was 1999, and I was in my second year of teaching 7th-grade social studies. Just one week into the year, two special education teachers approached me with a unique request: Would I be willing to welcome a student named Robbie into my homeroom and classroom?

Robbie was a student on the autism spectrum with high-functioning skills, but he had never been placed in a general education classroom. At that time, our collective understanding of autism was still evolving, and inclusive practices were far from the norm. It was uncharted territory for many of us (educators, students, and families alike).

I realized that for Robbie to succeed, he needed not only my support but also the support of his classroom peers. Our learning environment had to offer the specialized structure he required, and I understood that my students would look to my actions as a model. It was important that I demonstrated the same level of patience, understanding, support, and encouragement for Robbie that I aimed to show to every student.

To begin building that foundation, I met privately with a few classroom leaders to share more about Robbie's needs and to ask for their help in easing his transition. I approached them by acknowledging their strong leadership and their influence within our classroom community. I trusted they would rise to the occasion, and they—and subsequently the remainder of students—did.

What I remember most about that year was my students' ability to meet my expectations of building a classroom with a culture of empathy, respect, and inclusion. From day one, my students embraced Robbie without hesitation. I vividly remember the day a group of older students began to tease him in the hallway. My homeroom students didn't wait for an adult to intervene; they stood up for him instantly, letting others know that Robbie was part of their community.

Robbie thrived. He laughed, learned, built friendships, and experienced what every child deserves: to feel seen, supported, and valued. At the end of the year, Robbie gave me a small trophy that read "#1 Classroom Ever." I still keep that trophy in my office today. It's more than just a keepsake. It's a symbol of what's possible when we lead with heart, believe in the potential of every child, and provide high-support for every student to succeed in meeting high expectations.

The impact of that experience changed me forever. It redefined what I believed was possible when you provide high-quality support for every student. It also ignited my lifelong passion for inclusive education and student-centered leadership. It taught me that standing for a student isn't a moment; it's a mindset.

Today, when I present around the country on leadership, I often share a session called "Stand for a Student." And when it comes time to give an example of what that really means, I talk about Robbie. He wasn't just a student I supported and stood for. He was a student who changed the way I lead, teach, and think about the power of community.

CHAPTER 3

EXPECT Students to Aim High with Academics

A colleague shared this story with us: *She was the principal of a well-regarded public high school known for its academic rigor, wide range of learning opportunities, and strong arts program. The school served a fairly professional, affluent, and educated community. Many students took advanced courses, including numerous Advanced Placement classes. Most graduates who pursued higher education were accepted into well-known, respected universities.*

One day, a former high-achieving student, home on break from a prestigious university, called and asked to speak to the staff. The principal gladly arranged it, knowing most teachers had taught or known him. However, his message was not what anyone expected.

He explained that, although he had done well in high school, earning top grades and excelling in advanced classes, college had been a shock. He'd thought he was both academically and emotionally prepared but quickly realized he was not. The depth of thinking, level of complexity, and independence required were far greater than he had experienced before. While he appreciated the education he'd received, he admitted that learning had always come easily, so he hadn't been truly challenged to struggle, think deeply, or push past his comfort zone.

He encouraged the staff to reflect on this and to consider how they might better prepare students like him, not just for success in high school but also for the challenges ahead. As he put it, "In high school, I was a big toad in a small pond. But when I got to college, I discovered I was a small toad in a very big pond. I wasn't expecting to learn that."

Aiming high means believing in each student's capacity for growth and then creating the conditions that make that growth possible. Sadly, even well-intentioned teachers may believe they are providing a great education when, in reality, they are missing the mark. Aiming high isn't about assigning more work or making lessons harder; it's about believing that every student can develop and grow the skills of analyzing, synthesizing, evaluating, and applying knowledge. It also means helping students experience the satisfaction of working toward goals that are both challenging and achievable based on their individual abilities, strengths, and needs. In aiming high, we find the right combinations of content, practices, and support that will encourage each student to grow at rates and in areas beyond what has been the norm for that student.

When aiming high in academics, there is no ceiling. For some students, mastering grade-level expectations is a high aim (see Chapter 4). But good teachers don't make that the ultimate standard. Just because students reach or exceed grade-level standards doesn't mean they can't aim higher. In too many cases, students who are "top performers" are capable of aiming much higher but aren't provided with supports needed to enable this. Researchers who have found that up to 45% of American students score at least a year above grade level refer to these as "the invisible students."[1] All students are deserving of equal academic challenge and support to boost their academic proficiency.

We do recognize that some students have significant cognitive disabilities, and certain instructional practices may not apply in the same way for them. However, the vast majority of students (and even for those with diverse learning needs) are capable of growth, improvement, and success at reaching high standards when goals are appropriately tailored to the individual.

Put It Into Practice

Develop Deep Thinkers

In our role as educators, we have an obligation to help students learn to carefully consider, question, and understand things. Deep thinking is a route to more thorough understanding and greater meaning. Just as we challenge students and provide rigorous learning by nudging them to dig further into a question or topic and reach a bit beyond where they are now, we also train them to *think* a little deeper than they might initially.

Learning to think deeply is an intentional effort to deliberately analyze problems and situations that need more exploration. It involves plenty of curiosity, empathy, and self-awareness. Unlike quick decision-making or on-your-feet thinking (which are also necessary in life), deep thinking is a slow, scrutinizing, and reflective process. It's important that we provide students opportunities to develop and practice deep thinking in multiple ways:

+ Define and discuss the concept of deep thinking with students. Explain it as going beyond what is easy to see or think of and trying to discover more of the truth about something. (A smooth-talking, clever character in a story may seem trustworthy and caring, but careful reading and attention to the character's actions can give clues to a different persona. Or, an obvious explanation for trees dying in an area might be a beetle infestation. Considering other causes might reveal a complex set of weather, land management, or other issues that contributed to the problem.) You can also describe it as a process of thoughtful analysis (examining all the parts of something carefully to see what each part contributes to the whole and how they work together). Students think deeply when they:

+ Analyze, evaluate, and synthesize information.
+ Consider causes, consequences, and multiple solutions.
+ Make evidence-based decisions and predictions.
+ Question assumptions, compare perspectives, and think divergently.
+ Express understanding creatively.
+ Extend learning.
+ Make connections and notice relationships among ideas or elements.

+ Push students toward deeper thinking. In discussing historical figures, the teacher asks, *What makes someone a great leader?* This kind of question sets a context for a deeper dive into the study of leadership. Students quickly answer along the lines of *They're brave, They help people,* or *They make a difference.*

The teacher responds, *Those are great answers, but let's take a few moments to think more about this. Can someone be brave and still make poor decisions?* Using the "think-pair-share" strategy, students reflect individually, discuss with a partner, and then share thoughts in a class discussion. Based on group responses, he continues with *Let's take Martin Luther King, Jr., for example. Were his actions because he was brave or because he was being reckless?*

He then asks students to break into groups and discuss their thoughts while he circulates and encourages them to expand on their own thinking: *What evidence supports your idea? Could someone disagree? Why? Is there another example that fits or challenges that pattern?*

By the end of the lesson, student responses evolve beyond the basics. They begin to say things like, *A great leader is someone who thinks about consequences before acting,* or *Leadership means courage and wisdom, not just power.*

He ends by letting them know, *Today, you all exhibited deep thinking. You started with quick answers, but then you asked yourselves Why? and How? That's what real learning looks like.*

- Provide frequent opportunities for students to think deeply. This may sound too complex for some students or classes, but even our youngest students can deepen their thinking. This is not done through add-on lessons but is instead integrated into all learning experiences:

  - Build an environment that is safe for deep thinking. Be aware of the social and emotional dynamic that exists for students as you work to help them to think deeply. Many students are used to looking for the "right" response they think the teacher is seeking and fear that any divergent answers will displease the teacher. Developing deeper thinking can only work within a classroom culture that supports taking risks and that provides soft landings for misunderstandings and embarrassing moments. Let students know that mistakes, false notions, and blind alleys are steppingstones to deeper learning.

  - Teach students such terms as *reasoning, analyze, synthesize, reflection, evaluate, assumptions, conclusions,* and *perspective,* adapting explanations and examples to the grade level and giving them the opportunity to demonstrate understanding of the terms.

  - Ask students to provide examples of situations for deep thinking. They can consider how they use some of these deep-thinking skills in video games they play (thinking ahead to what results might be of a certain action; trying different ways to get past an obstacle or solve a problem; looking back at what caused an unwanted outcome; or using a new approach to start over and try again after a failure).

- Make open-ended questioning a habit. Model this practice, and teach students to do this as well. Constantly ask such questions as: *What caused this? What are the effects? What difference does this make, and why does it matter? Where else have you seen this? Knowing what happened already, what could happen next? How does this fit into a bigger picture? What's another way to say this (or solve this)? What can you infer about the author's beliefs? How (or who) might this help or hurt?* (Consult Erik Francis's *Now That's a Good Question!* and his other helpful books on questioning that deepens students' thinking.)

- In addition to modeling the asking of such questions, also show students ways to respond to not having a successful answer immediately. Show students that this is OK. Instead of feeling bad about themselves, they can use their indecision or uncertainty to help them decide what to do next.

- Expose students to information and concepts from many perspectives so that they interact with a variety of theories, viewpoints, and ideas. This can be challenging in today's social/political/cultural environment, so we encourage you to follow relevant policies of your school.

- Plan for the time, setting, and outcomes of deep thinking. When you ask students to think deeply, allow time for them to do so. Scrutinizing, analyzing, considering questions, following curiosity, being creative, reflecting, exploring, and pushing beyond your initial instincts takes time and practice. Work in increments with students to develop this. Provide an environment with limited distractions to allow for concentration. This includes serious focus and conversation on how extensive interaction with screens and social media tends to limit deeper thinking, and in many cases, provides a false sense that learning happened. And finally, help students realize that this is not just about isolated thinking. **Deep thinking leads to actions.** Much of their deliberation results in a decision about what to do next and how to do it. (For older students, having them think through whether to make that social media post can be a powerful exercise.) Students become more curious, open-minded, self-aware, and tolerant of other perspectives. Offer time for students to verbalize the outcomes that follow from their deep thinking.

Make Rigor Part of the Learning Culture and Mindset

Rigor has been an educational buzzword and goal for the past few decades. It's been championed as a major component in the push for students to reach high expectations. Unfortunately, the term *rigor* connotes stiffness, discomfort, extreme difficulty, or harsh inflexibility. And in many educational institutions, a dedication to this type of rigor has translated into giving students more work, harder tasks, longer projects, and expecting attainment of hundreds of rigid standards. But rigor has often been misunderstood; for while it may include or champion cognitive challenge (at its best), it can also be something far more flexible, active, and balanced than many have come to view and practice it.

As part of their definition of rigor, Douglas Fisher, Nancy Frey, and James Marshall (authors of *Rigor Unveiled*), point out that rigor "involves teaching, learning, and assessment processes that encourage students to understand deeply, think critically, and apply knowledge in complex, novel, and meaningful ways."[2] A rigorous culture is one in which components of this definition develop and thrive. The culture engages students in challenging learning possibilities and assignments that develop creativity and critical thinking instead of recall, draw students to explore and stretch beyond standards, support student autonomy in directing their own learning, and help them find purpose, value, and connections in what they learn.

Instead of mistaking rigor for just complex academic content and exacting standards, envision a culture of rigor as a catalyst for deep learning. Rigor in this sense is alive and invigorating. And it is not just for advanced or older students. It is for everyone, in all educational settings, at all grade levels. Similar in structure and function to high expectations and deeper learning, a culture of rigor combines challenge for students with masterful support. Here are some actions that contribute to building such a culture of rigor:

Similar in structure and function to high expectations and deeper learning, a culture of rigor combines challenge for students with masterful support.

- Provide a safe, predictable, un-chaotic setting that supports students as they explore, take risks, fail, and start over. Students need an environment in which they are comfortable to "stretch" and "dig deeper." Let them know that every day they'll be pushing themselves to understand deeply and to try new things. Regularly remind them of the many complex things they've already accomplished and learned. Part of a safe environment is the presence of trusting relationships. Students need teachers who value and care for them and who make efforts to promote positive, collaborative peer relationships.
- Make purpose a priority. Rigor challenges students to think deeply, widely, and creatively. Knowing the purpose for what they are doing (and struggling to understand) tells them why it matters. Take the time to ask, discuss, share, and verbalize the purpose of any learning activity.

+ Consistently set up learning tasks that require a reach in order to learn something new. Make sure students have clear instructions and appropriate resources to assist their challenging work. Students will find satisfaction with and new skills mastered and overcome as a result of their struggle. They need the support of your strategic scaffolding strategies and peer collaborations to ensure success in these tasks.

+ Foster autonomy. Self-reliance and ownership of learning is a key part of rigor. Provide many opportunities for students to work on their own—with support from quality resources, organizational tools, relevant peer interaction, and other sources of assistance.

+ Teach the levels of higher order thinking (remember, understand, apply, analyze, evaluate, create) and how they work together so students learn that each level has a purpose. You might use a trusted system of thinking levels such as the revision of Bloom's Taxonomy of Educational Objectives or Webb's Depth of Knowledge.[3] Higher order thinking in a 6th-grade science class where the standard focuses on ecosystems might look like this:

  + **Remember and recall facts:** Students must first be able to identify the different parts of an ecosystem, such as producers, consumers, scavengers, decomposers, how energy is transferred through those systems, effects on that system of the water cycle, factors that limit the system from working, and how that ecosystem interacts with surrounding ecosystems.

  + **Analyze and create:** Students can create an ecosystem and explain how it would operate. Alternatively, they can create ways to improve the health of a given ecosystem, or they can demonstrate the concept of an ecosystem and all its parts in a completely unrelated domain, such as the ecosystem of a library, a specific genre of books, or a family.

- **Apply ideas and use information in new ways:** Students can then predict what happens if one part of the ecosystem changes. They can find examples of changes within the ecosystem in which they live.

Promote Transfer of Learning

Transfer of learning occurs when someone applies knowledge or skills previously learned in one context to another context. Students can think of it as "moving" what they know to a new situation. (A 6th grader applies inquiry steps learned in science class to examining and analyzing an internet article presentation of a current social issue. Or a high-school student in a social studies class seeking to gain insights from graphs of changing population data in her state makes use of the skills of inference that she learned years ago when looking for clues to make decisions about characters in a story.)

Transfer fosters extension of learning, because something new is part of the thought and the task. It helps students understand the value of what they learn. (Math skills are useful far beyond math class: Understanding and calculating with money is part of financial management and planning. Math concepts related to measuring time, distance, and speed are needed for many life tasks such as travel and planning schedules.) Researchers David Perkins and Gavriel Salomon describe two types of transfer: *near transfer* (transfer among closely-related contexts or performances–using understanding of fractions when learning about ratio) and *far transfer* (transfer to different contexts and performances–climbing a ladder to climbing an ice waterfall).[4] Near transfer is more common and natural, while far transfer is more complex and requires explicit teaching to make connections and more use of higher order thinking skills. Students need many experiences with both kinds of learning transfer. When they apply previous knowledge to a new situation, they stretch their minds and broaden understanding beyond the original knowledge or skill.

Transfer of learning doesn't happen by chance. Students need a solid and meaningful foundation in skills, content, concepts, and strategies before any knowledge can be transferred. Teach for depth of understanding. As students understand how and why something works, it will be more easily adaptable to a new situation. If a student does simple division mechanically—just knowing that 15 divided by 5 = 3 (because he knows that 5 x 3 = 15)—that understanding of division is not helpful when it comes to dividing fractions. If he understands from 3rd grade that dividing 15 cupcakes by 5 is finding how many groups of 5 cupcakes can be found in the group of 15, then in middle school that understanding will help him with the tricky task of depicting a solution to 18 divided by 2/3, showing that there are 27 portions the size of 2/3 within 18.

To your work of previous knowledge with students, add explicit teaching, scaffolding, discussion, modeling, and, together, working out examples of both reflexive and mindful transfer.[5] Practice transfer over time, building metacognitive skills to help students recognize what they know and how to apply it to new contexts. Talk about what they are learning and how it is useful. As students grow and gain experience, their ability to transfer will deepen and become more sophisticated. They will feel the excitement and satisfaction of discovering how what they already know can expand to help them learn or master something new. This gives further meaning and motivation to their learning.

During my (Patti's) first year as an elementary teacher (after four years as an elementary music specialist), David was in my class. He was exceptionally bright and excelled in every subject, especially math. He grasped 5th-grade concepts easily, finished his work quickly, and often moved on to math puzzles and enrichment activities provided. I sensed he was bored, but since he was well-behaved, stayed busy, and didn't complain, I let things continue as they were.

One Friday afternoon, as the day ended, David asked me what I knew about trigonometry. I laughed and admitted that I'd taken it in high school but barely remembered anything beyond triangles and something called sine, cosine, and tangent. He just shrugged and said goodbye.

Monday morning, he burst into the classroom, eyes bright with excitement. Over the weekend, he found his father's old college trigonometry textbook and spent hours exploring it. He eagerly explained what sine, cosine, and tangent meant and how they were used in real life. My heart sank. I realized I had been so focused on covering the 5th-grade curriculum that I hadn't truly challenged a student who was more than ready to be stretched and inspired.

From that point on, I worked with David to create an individualized, accelerated math plan. He progressed through the required content at his own pace and then explored more advanced topics that sparked his interest. The following year, when I was assigned to teach 6th grade, I was fortunate to have him again. This time, I set up a more rigorous individualized program for him, including regular mentoring sessions with a high school math teacher to support his continued growth. It was a lesson I've never forgotten: meeting students where they are is important, but so is recognizing when they're ready to soar beyond.

CHAPTER 4

EXPECT Students to Succeed with Grade-Level Instruction

An administrator colleague shared this story with us: *Marie had a learning disability. Her teacher insisted that Marie could not learn the required 8th-grade math standards because, without accommodations, she struggled with addition, subtraction, multiplication, and division. Noticing that these skills had challenged Marie for several years, the teacher believed that until Marie could demonstrate fluency with the four fundamental operations, she could not possibly move forward with more complex 8th-grade math content, such as linear functions and algebraic expressions.*

It is with this firm conviction that the teacher's plan for Marie involved her repeated removal from her regular classroom for sessions to focus solely on basic math facts. This practice isolated Marie from her 8th-grade peers and severely limited her exposure to grade-level standards. After numerous conversations with the teacher about the need for grade-level content and many examples of success with grade-level teaching in similar situations, I finally convinced the teacher to try a change of course. The teacher taught grade-level content as the core of Marie's learning plan. At the same time, Marie took part in some remediation. But this was in addition to grade-level teaching, rather than in place of it. Once this change was implemented, Marie began to grow alongside her peers.

What was most remarkable to Marie, herself, as well as to her teacher and caregivers, was the speed of her significant progress. She gained a functional understanding of many complex 8th-grade concepts while continuing to work on foundational math skills. This approach required more teacher time and careful scheduling and more time and practice from Marie, but the academic—and social—benefits far outweighed the challenges.

While we have been focusing on high expectations, we need to emphasize that, **for many students, grade-level standards ARE the high standards they need to reach.** Too many students have not experienced the satisfaction of meeting grade-level expectations. Building a culture of high expectations means supporting and cheering students on as they work to master grade-level standards. This does not mean stopping there, nor does it mean students cannot also aim for the higher-level expectations as discussed in Chapter 3.

We've never met a teacher who claims to hold low expectations. Yet teachers often work so hard to remediate what students do not know that they sometimes fall short of offering students experiences with grade-level content, concepts, and skills that they need. A 2018 study found that only 44% of teachers believed their students could meet state standards, resulting in less than one-third of class time spent on grade-level instruction.[1] This widespread "catch-up" approach limits progress, because in order to advance to higher levels of learning, students need exposure to grade-level learning tasks, materials, content, and instruction. With the right support, grade-level instruction gives all students access to meaningful learning. (See more about meaningful learning in Chapter 12.) Research shows students given grade-level assignments "struggled less and learned more" than peers who received lower-level remediation instead.[2]

This does not mean that we never review previously-learned content, build up skills from previous years, or teach something a student missed entirely. Remember that grade-level standards and expectations are arbitrary. They are the conclusions educators have come to about what 3rd graders or 11th graders have to learn. The grade-level categories are convenient for planning and record-keeping. There are plenty of 9th graders operating with 4th-grade understanding or skill sets in one area but 8th-grade level in another and different grade levels altogether in yet another. Good teaching often includes re-visiting some of the previous year's curriculum while setting the context for the next year's material.

Put It Into Practice

Ensure Experiences with Grade-Level Skills and Materials

Instruction in grade-level content and skills ensures that all students have access to a high-quality education. Simply placing students in the same room and teaching the same standards is not enough. The learning environment must be designed to meet a wide range of needs while maintaining grade-level (or higher) expectations for all. Many students may need some remediation along the way, but the intent should be to avoid "meeting students where they are" and simply keeping them there. For struggling students like Marie (from the story above), learning alongside typical-aged peers in an inclusive, intentional, and well-supported classroom—with personalized instruction, scaffolds, and interventions in place—offers significant academic and social-emotional benefits.

The following actions are starting points for ensuring that all students (even those who show that they've missed or not been able to master some skills or understand some concepts from previous grades) are exposed to grade-level material:

+ Understand the benefits of teaching grade-level standards to students who are not already meeting them. Doing so:
    + Communicates the teacher's belief in every student's potential and shows that all learners are capable of achieving rigorous goals.
    + Increases engagement of students when they are involved with content and concepts suited to their developmental readiness, interests, and skills they will need in the future.
    + Diminishes self-consciousness, self-doubt, and shame about being "behind" on competencies. However, if students are experiencing shame because they struggle academically, engaging them with grade-level material and skills is only part of the solution. Any instructional approach will be effective only within a classroom culture where students and adults are equally valued and mutually accepting of one another and where students are supported in seeing themselves as capable.
    + Fosters self-confidence and belief that they can achieve rigorous goals and reach grade-level expectations.
    + Builds knowledge and skills in a logical progression, preparing students for future success in post-secondary education, careers, and life.
    + Supports consistency across classrooms, schools, and the district, ensuring every student receives instruction aligned with state and national standards.
    + Helps close achievement gaps by holding high expectations for all learners, regardless of background or "readiness."
    + Enables better monitoring of student progress, allowing teachers to provide additional support or acceleration as needed based on common standards.
+ Plan for grade-level instruction. Start by using grade-level standards and expectations as your foundation. Understand the details of each standard, and plan learning experiences and

assignments to meet these. Know the standards students were expected to master in the prior grade and how the current standards connect to and prepare them for more advanced expectations in later grades. Use grade-level texts and materials relevant to students' ages and interests. Provide tools and manipulatives that support access to grade-level concepts. Adjust instruction as needed to nudge, support, or boost student progress, but keep grade-level expectations as the goal. **Ensure teacher-made assessments align to grade-level standards.**

+ Re-teach when necessary. Sometimes there is a clear need to re-teach, or teach for the first time, some foundational content needed for the student to understand new content that calls for a mini-lesson right there in class. While exposing the student to grade-level content and standards, you can certainly use resources or re-teach standards from earlier grade levels to provide the needed foundation, as long as the material is developmentally appropriate for the student. Some educators now describe this remediation effort as learning acceleration, an approach that begins with grade-appropriate content and strategically adds scaffolding only when students need it to master grade-level work. Others refer to it as "just-in-time teaching" or "just-in-time interventions." This approach ensures that students spend more time engaged in grade-level tasks (an essential factor in helping them catch up.)[3] When heading into a 7th-grade lesson on the function and processes of the cell membrane, the 7th-grade science teacher (not wanting to delay exposing students to the 7th-grade material), introduces all students to the 7th-grade curriculum content on cell membrane processes. For some students who need some catch-up to enable them to work with the new concepts, she does a quick review of relevant cell parts and structure. (See more on scaffolding in Chapter 2.)

Prioritize and Pace Content

With dozens of standards in each course or grade level (and too little instructional time to give full effort to all of them) many schools are prioritizing content standards. This is a process of selecting a subset of standards in a course or content area that will receive the most instructional focus.

In my (Laurie's) school district, we spent several years intentionally identifying priority standards and developing proficiency scales for each grade level and subject area. Our 8th-grade math teacher, who has over two decades of math teaching experience, examined the twenty-eight state content standards for 8th-grade mathematics. In collaboration with high school educators who contributed their experience about what students need to know when entering high school math, he identified twelve as priority standards for students. These were prioritized because of their foundational necessity to higher-level math and long-term application to other mathematical processes and topics. Once the priority standards were established, he was ready to develop additional curriculum supports to help students reach grade-level standards. Focusing on twelve priority standards does not mean the remaining standards are overlooked or untaught. Instead, he integrates them into the instruction of the identified priorities to ensure comprehensive coverage. (Although the standard "Know and apply properties of integer exponents to generate equivalent numerical expressions" is not a priority, he introduces or reviews it (and works examples) as base knowledge needed for the three priority standards that involve solving linear equations.) Here are some suggestions for prioritizing and pacing:

- Follow your school or district procedures for identifying **priority standards**. It is best to work with colleagues teaching similar subject matter. A vertical examination of the standards and discussion with teachers of other grade levels gives a broader view of how standards connect to those that come before and after them. Identify your criteria for prioritization. Generally, schools prioritize standards that are essential for success in a course or unit, those covering skills and knowledge that last beyond one topic or test or are foundational to future learning, and those that are applicable across topics, content areas, or grade levels.

- Develop a **proficiency scale** for each priority standard. Teachers who will use the scales should develop these in collaboration. This process clearly defines criteria to determine a student's proficiency level on that standard. These scales are used to provide targeted guidance to support and evaluate progress toward grade-level expectations, especially for students performing below grade level. (Negotiating descriptors of proficiency with colleagues is a sensitive task. You might want to have a few jokes and snacks on hand to relax everyone for these meetings!) Remember that scales and rubrics may be used for teachers to determine grades or progress, but they are even more valuable for students to self-monitor their progress toward a learning target. Therefore, be sure that these tools are user-friendly for and shared with students.

- Establish a pacing guide. Use a **pacing or scope-and-sequence guide** to ensure all students have the opportunity to master grade-level content within the school year. While it's natural to support students who struggle, we must be careful not to "love them to death" by over-scaffolding or slowing instruction to the point that it deprives them of access to essential learning. However, in reality, there are some students who learn faster than others in certain units of study and some who are really challenged by a particular unit of study. If we want to keep things moving forward so as not to fall out of sync with our pacing guide, but a student has not mastered something, we have one of three choices: First, if it's something we can weave into the context of the next unit or one down the road, it's OK to move on, but let's just make sure we weave it into that later study. Second, if it's something that's just nice to know but not germane or a first or second priority standard, let it go; it's not worth the teacher-student dysfunction that sometimes happens when fighting for something so insignificant. Finally, if it's too fundamental/pivotal for the learning ahead to let it go, then we're going to have to stay a bit longer with it, possibly delaying the sequence slightly as we make sure it's mastered.

Know When to Accommodate or Modify

Understanding the difference between *accommodations* and *modifications* is essential to helping struggling students learn grade-level content. These legal terms, their definitions, and implications are geared to special education. An accommodation provides additional support or adjustments to make it possible for a student to still tackle the same expectations in a class or subject. A modification alters what the student is expected to learn. In short, accommodations impact how a student learns; modifications impact what a student learns. In a science lesson, students might read a text explaining the structure and causes of three types of volcanoes and create a chart comparing and contrasting them. An **accommodation** for a student who struggles with reading could include having the same grade-level text read aloud and providing a structured compare-and-contrast template. The student is still learning the same content and meeting the same standard.

> In short, accommodations impact how a student learns; modifications impact what a student learns.

A **modification** would involve changing the learning expectation itself such as providing a simplified text that reduces or omits key information about how volcanoes form, so the student is no longer required to fully compare the causes and structures as outlined in the standard.

Accommodations are generally written within a student's Individualized Education Plan (IEP) or 504 plan; they focus on how a student is taught and/or assessed, not on what the student is expected to learn. All students are taught the same grade-level standards and take the same standardized assessments aligned to those standards. Accommodations simply allow students to access learning and demonstrate understanding in different ways. It is important that accommodations be **routinely used in instruction** before being used on state assessments. Student IEP or 504 plans usually have accommodations **in how content is delivered** to students (text-to-speech for directions, items, or passages; staff reader for directions; large-print materials; simplified/repeated directions; magnification devices, etc.), **in how students demonstrate knowledge** (speech-to-text/dictation, an adult scribe, use of calculator, graphic organizers, etc.), **in their setting** (small-group, individual, separate location, noise-canceling headphones, etc.), and **in time allowed** (extended time, frequent breaks, etc.).

Modifications change **what is taught and provided for students** with an IEP that clearly specifies the need for alterations. When modifications are in place, students do not receive instruction on the full set of grade-level standards. As outlined in the IEP, these students participate in alternative assessments rather than the standard grade-level assessments. Typically, only a very small percentage of students qualify for modifications.

Students with these plans sometimes need additional, appropriate support when learning grade-level content. Their IEP or 504 plans spell out the legally-required support. Over the years, we have seen some teachers over accommodate or inappropriately modify grade-level standards to help a student experience success in a classroom learning task. We have noticed cases where the specific accommodations or modifications have not been approved as part of the student's plan. Sometimes teachers provide in-class accommodations that are not allowed on standardized assessments or progress-monitoring assessments. When these are not available to students during testing, they do poorly. In addition, over-doing these or using them where they are not prescribed minimizes the chances of building support that can help students become independent.

Although accommodations and modifications are intended for special education, we also sometimes see them used inappropriately with students in the general education setting. For those students who struggle, scaffolding is an appropriate strategy to support learning, build skills, and promote independence. (Of course, this does not mean that we don't use scaffolding for students with disabilities, too.) Accommodations and modifications, however, should be reserved for students with IEPs or 504 Plans, where they are legally defined and required. When teachers overuse accommodations or modifications, it is usually done with good intentions and a genuine desire to help. Still, these practices can unintentionally distort a student's true performance and understanding. If a student's grade does not accurately reflect mastery of a standard, it can influence factors beyond the classroom, such as:

- Supports and services received (gifted and talented, intervention, and accommodation eligibility)
- Effectiveness of supports and accurate data for IEP, 504, and MTSS services
- Honors, awards, or scholarships
- Promotion and retention
- Athletic and extra-curricular eligibility

A teacher Laurie worked with noticed that his students consistently earned high class grades but performed poorly on final exams and standardized tests. When we reflected on why, he realized he was over-supporting (and accommodating when he should not) students on assignments and assessments. As a result, their grades suggested mastery even when they had not fully mastered the standards. His constant coaching during their classwork led them to depend on him to get them to the right answers rather than working through problems on their own to truly learn the math processes. He shifted his approach by providing more support during instruction and student practice rather than during graded work. He then used independent assignments and assessments to accurately gauge student understanding and identify gaps. This allowed him to reteach intentionally and reassess as needed. The results were clear: students learned more, their grades were accurate and improved, their standardized test scores matched those higher grade reports, and they were more successful in the next grade level.

In a discussion about teaching grade-level standards to students who are behind or struggling, our 8th-grade math teacher Alex and I (Laurie) reflected on how often students who struggled with math in previous grades can be successful on many 8th-grade math standards because these standards are often more about the process than computation.

We talked about a former 8th-grade student, Tom, who had slower processing abilities and was supported with an IEP. When included in a co-taught 8th-grade math class (serving students in both general education and special education), Tom was able to become proficient in many 8th-grade priority standards and near proficient in most others.

Once he understood the process of solving an equation with one variable, the only question Alex would have to ask him was, "What do we do next?" It was the first time Tom had felt success in math. And, as Alex noted, "Many times, success or that feeling of being successful will just instill confidence in a student, and feeling confident is more than half the battle. Don't we want that same confidence for all students, even those not on grade-level?"

CHAPTER 5

EXPECT Students to Give and Receive Meaningful Feedback

I (Laurie) began my education career as a high school English teacher. The summer before my third year, my principal asked if I would teach 12th-grade AP English Literature and Composition. It was a dream come true, especially since my own AP English teacher had inspired me to enter the profession. I eagerly attended a College Board Summer Institute and came back ready for the challenge.

One of the biggest challenges I faced in teaching AP English was helping students write and accept feedback on timed, free-response essays. Each week, they wrote an in-class forty-minute essay, and I spent hours assessing them and providing feedback. The more essays I scored, the more confident I felt, and in my first year our class average pass rate on the AP exam was well above the national average.

But many of my high-achieving students struggled to accept anything less than top scores. These students were among the highest performing in the school and accustomed to top grades, so anything less was difficult for them to accept. I worked hard to build credibility, providing multiple re-do *opportunities for full credit (which I credit for the high AP pass rates), but despite offering that option, skepticism lingered. Their writing, analytical skills, and ability to support an argument still needed work, even if they couldn't see it. Parents called. Students complained. While the multiple revision (and improved grade) opportunities helped, many still did not fully trust the feedback or their grade.*

To build trust, I reached out to experienced AP colleagues and arranged for outside teachers to score some essays. I promised to honor the higher score. Once they saw that external evaluations almost always matched mine, confidence grew almost overnight, and students and parents began trusting the process.

I could have been offended, defensive, or insisted students simply "accept" their grades, but my goal was for them to process and truly use the feedback. Having other professionals support this process made a significant difference, for me and for the students. That experience taught me that feedback, no matter how thoughtful, is useless if students don't understand or trust it. I began spending more time teaching students how to interpret and apply feedback and helping them identify strengths, weaknesses, and ways to self-assess. In doing so, it strengthened their ability to effectively use feedback, which in turn strengthened their writing.

Feedback is information given to someone about a performance or product. It can be formal (planned, scheduled) or casual (brief, impromptu). It can be written or spoken, be delivered in various ways (notes on assignments, conferences, brief comments, discussions, students comparing their own work with exemplars and noting differences and similarities), and come from different sources (teacher to student, peer to peer, parent to student, or student to teacher). Overall, the purpose of any feedback is to help someone grow. It allows the learner to gain responses and insights from someone, think about one's own progress or behavior, and gain new understandings to improve on or learn something important.

Done well, feedback is a dynamic tool for growth toward high standards and improved performance. It affirms effort, gives explicit guidance for improving performance, and energizes learners to continue to work hard with renewed dedication and move forward.[1] As students listen to feedback, determine what is useful, and apply it to improve their work, they engage in decision-making. They use critical thinking skills such as analyzing and synthesizing, along with creative thinking, to find new ways to present their ideas. Because they are the final decision-makers about how to use the feedback they receive, they also build agency (the empowerment to take an active role and ownership in their own learning), which strengthens their confidence and independence.

Put It Into Practice

Give Students Feedback that Really Works

Effective feedback is one of the most powerful tools teachers have for fostering growth. It should help students clearly understand what they're doing well, what needs improvement, and how to move forward. It must be substantive and meaningful enough for students to understand, consider, and apply to their work. Before you give feedback to students and teach them about feedback:

- Plan clear guidelines for feedback. To further growth and learning, feedback should:
  - Be aligned with learning goals and clear criteria. Students should understand exactly what aspect of their work is being addressed. (If the assignment is to show steps you took in estimating the solution to a math problem, don't focus feedback on the final answer or the spelling. Instead, praise steps that clearly worked as accurate estimation strategies and guide the student in identifying any steps where inaccurate estimation may have led to a wrong answer.)

- Be specific and actionable. (See the "Avoid empty feedback" section below.) Offer concrete, developmentally appropriate next steps for improvement, and empower the student to take those steps without help. Then give the student an opportunity to be assessed anew (for full credit).
- Be honest, but kind. Provide truthful feedback that encourages growth without discouraging or demeaning the student. (*These sections of your timeline have clear labels that tell what was happening. Could you apply that same clarity and depth of information to this section, too?*)
- Be objective and criterion-based. Describe the work according to established standards, not personal opinions or subjective judgments. (Instead of *The opening paragraph is weak,* say, *Notice the rubric description of qualities for an effective opening paragraph. Compare yours to that. What changes would you like to make to bring it to that standard?*)
- Be hopeful and affirming. Share progress, improvement, and potential to motivate continued effort. (*Wow, with your changes, these paragraphs each have a convincing reason for your viewpoint. Apply that same approach to your last reason. You're almost there!*)
- Be fair and consistent. Address only the task requirements, and apply expectations uniformly across all students.
- Be collaborative. Engage students in reflecting on and participating in their own growth and improvement. Given a list of criteria for a specific type of assignment, students can meet in pairs to help one another compare their past and current work and help each other see improvement trends.
- Be timely and balanced. Give feedback soon enough to be useful with insight to guide learning without overwhelming the student.

When feedback meets these qualities, it builds trust and resilience and gives students substantive suggestions to help them move confidently toward mastery.

- Support and reinforce the feedback. Provide rubrics or other guides to help students understand the criteria and strategies for improvement, along with examples of strong work that model expectations. The purpose of rubrics is to help students monitor their own success toward a goal, so rubrics should be written in language and structure that show students' steps toward mastery. Students must be able to look at the rubric and determine where they are in the learning at a particular time. Give students time to reflect on the feedback, ask questions, and revise their work accordingly. Follow up to see whether the feedback helped them make progress, and take time to celebrate growth and improvements.

Avoid Empty Feedback

Over their years in school, most students have probably received a fair amount of feedback that hasn't been all that helpful. No matter how well-intentioned, vague or general comments will not lead to the powerful learning that is possible from quality feedback. Feedback is empty if it doesn't connect to the criteria for an expectation or doesn't move the work forward in a positive direction with real improvement.

Feedback is empty if it doesn't connect to the criteria for an expectation or doesn't move the work forward in a positive direction with real improvement.

+ Avoid feedback without substance. Whether comments are short descriptors, complete sentences, positive, or encouraging improvement, they must be specific, directly aligned to criteria, and include prompts for future action. Such comments as these below are affirming and show excitement about performance, but they are not accompanied by specifics: questions, suggestions, or nudges that lead students to understand what actions they can take to improve the performance:

> Good start
> The last part needs more work.
> Too brief, too short
> This is an improvement over your last report.
> Excellent work
> Doesn't meet the criteria
> Interesting word choice
> I loved your conclusion!
> You worked hard on this.
> This is your best explanation yet!
> Add more
> This shows good thinking.

+ Instead, use precise, descriptive feedback:
  - *You used onomatopoeia ("Crash!") in your opening sentence, and the sound of it caught my attention right away, which made me interested in reading more.*
  - *It appears you used a problem-solving strategy that didn't work for solving the proportion. Let's review that skill, and then you can apply it to the next three problems.*
  - *The ending of your science inquiry is missing a description of the experiment's final conclusions. Can you add that?*

+ *You cited several pieces of evidence to support your claim, just as the guidelines required. This builds your credibility on the position.*
+ *Your title caught my attention. I wanted to read your essay right away to find out what food will help me live forever!*
+ *Active verbs really gave power to your explanation. Let's circle those. Keep using that approach.*

Teach Students the Skills of Effective Feedback

Students also deserve multiple opportunities to give feedback to each other and to the teacher. But before students do this, make sure they are well-trained in the art of feedback. Receiving and completing observations and evaluations that are meaningful, appropriate, and helpful teaches students how to express themselves, advocate for themselves, uplift each other, and manage their own constructive responses when receiving critique or feedback. Students' insights and voice provide valuable information and learning for the teacher, too. Include these actions in teaching students to give, receive, and use feedback:

+ Provide students with written guidelines for giving feedback. Demonstrate the guidelines as you give feedback to students.
+ Suggest some opening sentence starters: *The picture captions give some clear facts about your topic. . . You may want to consider . . . The first two steps of your problem-solving explanation are clear. Take another look at the third one.* Ask students to contribute examples of responses that are effective feedback.
+ Address the social and emotional components of giving and hearing feedback. Students will readily understand that the process could be intimidating and that it's important to give feedback in ways that uplift, not discourage, each other. Discuss appropriate responses to feedback, especially when it's not as

positive as you hoped. Take advantage of student's insights on how to avoid being defensive, how to give feedback kindly and sensitively, and how to get the most out of feedback being given (such as by asking for clarification or more evidence to support the feedback). Role-play some feedback scenarios using hypothetical or anonymous work samples.

+ Remind students that they make the final decisions about what feedback to use and how to use it to make their product better. Suggest that they ask questions if they need clarification about the feedback and respectfully thank peers or the teacher for the feedback.

+ Teach students to limit feedback to just a few elements at a time. It is less overwhelming to respond to a few, resolve them, and then move on to a couple of others. Feedback is more manageable and meaningful if it is focused and limited. Try this simple "Glow and Grow" approach: Students join in pairs and give feedback to each other on a task or short assignment; they identify one thing the partner has done well (Glow) and one thing the partner can improve (Grow).

+ Let students sometimes choose who gives them feedback. When students are planning a project or report (or after they complete it), each student can ask specific individuals to review their work and provide comments. Reviewers can be classmates, a family member, another adult, or a student outside the class. Provide reviewers with criteria, and include a blank page (or feedback guide) at the end of the project. The feedback guide can give examples of helpful vs. unhelpful feedback.

+ See Chapter 14 on feedback students give to themselves, as we discuss self-reflection and self-evaluation for students. The principles of effective feedback connect strongly to students' reflection on their own work.

Invite Students to Give Feedback to the Teacher

You will become a better teacher when you hear and use input from your students. This process helps you see what and how they are learning, what is working, and how they perceive your teaching. It is another wonderful way to show students you believe in them and value their insights. Listening to student feedback allows you to polish or alter teaching practices and make other adjustments needed for better student learning. Students' feedback is a vital element for the teacher's formative assessment. The process of students contributing feedback to their teachers also honors student voices, empowers them to evaluate their own learning, and inspires deep thinking:

- Ask students what you do that works for them and what doesn't. *What should I keep doing, stop doing, or start doing?* These questions will likely result in input on a variety of teaching behaviors and actions (your lessons, level of connection with students, practices that do or do not engage students, strongest teaching techniques, consistency on classroom protocols, etc.). You can direct questions to specific topics or let students decide the directions of their answers.
- Try short check-in interviews. In the article, "Feedback Friday," teacher Nicole Greene describes how she sets aside part of her Friday class time for one-on-one interviews (one to five minutes) with each student. (Sometimes it happens digitally.) Each time she asks: *What went well for you this week? What can I do to help next week? What can I do to be a better teacher?* Green says the data she gets is "worth its weight in gold."[2]
- Ask students to write a letter to future students. Each student writes a letter to be given to a (random) student who comes into your class next year. The letter tells that next-year student how to be successful in your class. These can be anonymous. This will provide a wealth of feedback to you.

- Ask students to brainstorm the most significant units, topics, or concepts they studied the past year. Record their ideas on the board or on large sheets of chart paper. Then, give each student an amount of (hypothetical or toy) money or points–perhaps $100 or 100 points–to "spend" on the topics they found most valuable or engaging. Students can allocate their dollars or points in multiples of five, giving more to the units they liked best and less (or none) to others. When you add up totals for each topic, you'll quickly see which content students found most interesting, relevant, or meaningful.

- Act on the feedback you get from students. Their feedback is a waste of time if students don't see it making any difference. Respond to students. Tell them what you learned. Let them see your actions that show you listened, have regard for what they offered, and are using it to improve their learning experiences.

Tucked away in the pages of a yearbook more than fifty years old are three handwritten letters. School was not always easy for my (Patti's) husband Dan, but he worked hard, was athletic, and represented our high school in football and track. At the end of each season or year, he would receive a handwritten letter from his coach mailed to his home address.

1968 – Dear Dan, I appreciated your good attitude this year. Keep working on form and trying to improve your strength. Be ready for football this fall and have a nice summer.

1969 – Dear Dan, It was a most pleasing experience to have the opportunity to work with you and the other boys this fall. Your cooperative attitude and fine work habits made the season fly by too rapidly. Your offensive blocking at the 4 hole in the Willamette game looked very good. Keep up your fine attitude and working habits the rest of the school year. If you ever need a recommendation or reference for a job, please feel free to use my name.

1970 – Dear Dan, I appreciated your fine attitude and cooperation this year. I'm sorry you had to go to work because I know you would have shot putted over 50' before the season ended. The best of luck in your post-graduate years. Come back and see us from time to time and remember me if you ever need a reference or recommendation.

Receiving specific and meaningful feedback meant a lot 50+ years ago, and it still does today!

PART 2

Engage!

Introduction

WHAT?
A Picture of Engagement

Student engagement is at the heart of a meaningful and successful educational experience. It drives effective instruction, positive behavior, learning, and well-being. But perceptions of engagement can differ: some see it as students paying attention, some define it by students' investment in their work, while others see it as adding fun activities to spark interest.

In today's fast-changing, digital, and socially-complex world, traditional teaching alone rarely inspires enduring engagement, and content can seem disconnected from students' lives. Research, along with educators' experience, has shown that when we connect students with purposeful, relevant, and cohesive content, engagement increases, bringing academic, social, and emotional benefits. When engagement is missing, students lose opportunities for growth, satisfaction, and lasting learning.

Definition

Student engagement: the level of cognitive, physical, behavioral, and emotional involvement and intellectual investment students have in their learning processes; the level of student commitment and persistence to think deeply and understand, create, or master something difficult that matters

More about the Meaning of Student Engagement

Engagement is not something that the teacher does TO the student. It is the student's own connection, commitment, and involvement. While authentic student engagement can be fueled (or diminished) by what and how teachers teach, arrange, provide, and promote, at its roots, engagement is an intrinsic process that ultimately generates from within the student.

Simple definitions don't adequately convey the meaning of *student engagement*. For too long, we've used simple definitions of *engagement*, equating it with *participation* and *attention*. Research has helped us understand the multi-dimensional nature and deeper meanings of the term. We've learned that engagement can be cognitive, behavioral, or emotional. And we've learned that these forms may (and should) mix but that each is not the same as the other, and each is not the whole story.[1]

Engagement does not mean that a student is compliant, busy, or occupied. It is not just about coming to class, staying awake and alert, completing assignments, doing homework, cooperating with the group, taking part in discussions and activities, having a positive attitude, or showing enthusiasm for a topic. Yes, highly engaged students will likely exhibit these, because the actions are components of behavioral or emotional engagement, **but to further learning, full student engagement must include *cognitive* investment.** Such full engagement is about being committed to gaining something meaningful, about interacting with ideas and content that matter—something that arouses interest, curiosity, and passion in ways that inspire hard work, persistence, taking on challenges, deep thinking, and satisfaction.

Student engagement involves a dynamic interrelationship among the following three factors: the learning content or task (its quality, relevance, and challenge), **attributes of the student** (self-confidence, feelings of competence, fears, perseverance, work habits, accountability, past successes and failures, and belief that the task can be accomplished), **and the setting** (the level and quality of support from the surrounding class instruction and culture).

Engagement is not always dazzling. We do students a disservice if we try to make all learning activities entertaining. Cognitive engagement involves demanding work: thinking long and hard, grappling with setbacks, pushing through frustration, struggling with complicated concepts, stretching to meet a challenge that feels out of reach, trying multiple strategies, figuring out what something means or how to make something work, or starting over. Sometimes it is very quiet, too. And it's not always fun. But when students succeed at challenging tasks, there is plenty of joy and satisfaction.

Engagement and disengagement are not fixed states. Although some students may spend more time in one state or the other, anyone can move in and out of both. Engagement level is highly influenced and readily changed by such factors as different teachers, classes, subjects, topics, or learning activities. A student's state can change due to personal, family, or social situations, health, current events, time of day, amount of sleep, hormones, the latest text or social media post, or romance (or lack thereof).

WHY?
The Power of Engagement

Student engagement plays a vital and far-reaching role in education. When students are strongly engaged, they deeply connect—behaviorally, emotionally, socially, physically, and cognitively—to their learning. Engagement makes learning more personal and meaningful, encouraging students to take greater ownership and interest in their education.

Conversely, when students are disengaged or only minimally engaged, they lose these valuable benefits. Disengagement leaves them disconnected from their learning environment and unable to see the relevance or purpose of school.

Some Discoveries about Student Engagement

Countless research studies affirm the power of student engagement. Here are some of the most critical evidences to consider:[2]

> Engagement makes learning more personal and meaningful, encouraging students to take greater ownership and interest in their education.

1. There is a strong correlation between student engagement and academic outcomes.
2. As students get older, they report decreasing engagement and enjoyment in learning at school. Engagement levels decline during the middle school and high school years.
3. Parents and caregivers think students are more engaged in school than students report that they are.
4. Classroom management issues are significantly related to students' levels of engagement.
5. Levels of student engagement are strongly influenced by the learning culture, relevance, and appropriate challenge of the curriculum, quality and personal meaning of class content and educational experiences, support students receive for their work, and level of teacher engagement.
6. Disengagement is significantly influenced by boredom and frustration. One root cause of boredom or frustration is the lack of learning activities that are personally engaging (relevant, appropriate, challenging, content-rich, or content-relevant).

7. Engagement begets engagement. When students experience successes resulting from meaningful engagement, they are motivated to invest further.

8. A student's level of engagement in learning affects the student's long-term experiences and success in and beyond school.

Benefits of Student Engagement

Deep engagement changes the picture of learning for students with many positive effects. The research is clear. In classrooms with robust student engagement:[3]

- There is genuine and enthusiastic active participation in learning. Classrooms are livelier; students are inquisitive, inspired, and free to take on challenges.
- Students collaborate freely and meaningfully with peers.
- Classroom management is easier, with few behavior disruptions and many visible signs of care and respect for peers.
- Students build strong relationships and have a high sense of belonging, connection, and community.
- Students who are highly engaged in their learning:
  - Grow to higher levels of achievement and understand more deeply.
  - Show greater focus and retention of information, concepts, and processes.
  - Have fewer tardies, better attendance, and lower dropout rates.
  - Develop deeper thinking skills and verbalize and evaluate their own thinking.
  - Demonstrate and increase in independence, self-belief, intrinsic motivation, competence, and ownership of their learning.

- Are more likely to persist and don't give up as easily when challenged.
- Are free to be creative and to explore, create, and experiment.

The Problem of Student Disengagement

Some describe student disengagement as a widespread crisis or even a national epidemic, one that has persisted for years and worsened during and after the pandemic.[4] Schools recognize the urgent need to re-engage students who have become disconnected from their learning. While some factors contributing to disengagement are beyond educators' control, we can still identify its signs and create supportive school cultures that help students reconnect through proven strategies.

Disengagement can stem from expectations that are too high or too low, a lack of challenge or relevance in learning, feelings of incompetence or self-doubt, lack of belonging, or experiences such as bullying or discrimination. It can also be influenced by personal, family, social, or academic factors. And, it's impossible to work with students now and not notice the huge contribution to academic disengagement made by the inescapable draw of cell phones and social media. Educators must observe, listen, and respond early to uncover root causes and take action. Left unaddressed, disengagement severely weakens learning.[5]

Consequences of Student Disengagement

These behaviors are both indicators and consequences of disengagement (and often depression):

- Poor attendance; skipping class
- Barely showing up; doing sloppy work or just enough to get by
- Apathy, withdrawal, hopelessness, low energy, falling asleep
- Restlessness, poor concentration, easily distracted

+ Anxiety or fear (about things–in or out of school–including fear of failure)
+ Disinterest in classroom activities, resistance to involvement, or refusal to do work
+ Disruptive or impulsive behavior, including making choices to participate in risky behaviors

Disengaged students may:

+ Get good grades but do as little as possible.
+ Believe they can't succeed at a particular class, subject, concept, or task.
+ Feel powerless to have any control over their school life or learning.
+ Perceive or experience lack of peer support or teacher support.
+ Not be able to see learning as relevant to their lives or having any meaning.
+ Think that they don't need to learn what's being taught.
+ Drop out.

HOW?
The Pathway to Engagement

How can educators make use of the powers of engagement? How do we ignite the fire that fuels students' investment in learning and help them move toward deeper, sustained engagement?

The desire to increase student engagement requires us to further clarify and illustrate what engagement is and is not. It also calls us to consider the teacher's passion and enthusiasm for the subject, to create safe classrooms where students experience genuine belonging and community, and to provide opportunities for them to explore meaningful interests and express their creativity. In Part 2 of the book, we explore these elements of student engagement and more through **belonging, peer interaction, compelling content, active learning experiences, and exploration.** Each of the following chapters (6-10) describes a specific, concrete action with supporting strategies to spark, nurture, and sustain engagement. The recommended behaviors and practices are observable to our students, ourselves, and others. They can be intentionally practiced, honed, and, in many cases, measured.

Although Part 2 focuses on engagement, you'll find that the attitudes and practices here that deepen engagement also facilitate and strengthen the processes of reaching high **expectations.** As well, when students are invested in their learning and are committed to working hard on something about which they are passionate, they become more **empowered.**

CHAPTER 6

ENGAGE Students with Belonging

*I*t was hard not to love Sunni. I met her during my first year as super-intendent, when she was a 1st grader with Prader-Willi syndrome—a rare genetic condition that affects physical, cognitive, and behavioral development.

That year, our preschool–8th-grade district began implementing inclusive learning environments, a powerful strategy for supporting students with disabilities by blending general and special education through co-teaching. This collaborative approach to instruction helped us provide least restrictive environments for all students, including those in specialized programs. Sunni thrived in this inclusive environment.

When her mother Janice hand-delivered an 8th-grade celebration announcement thanking the staff members who had supported Sunni since preschool and I saw my own name listed, I felt deeply moved.

As a superintendent, it's far more difficult to build close relationships with students than it was when I served as a principal, assistant principal, teacher, or coach. Yet one of the great privileges of this role is witnessing the long arc of a student's growth. Seeing Sunni walk across the stage at the 8th-grade celebration was a truly special moment. In many other circumstances, a student with Sunni's specific needs might not have had the opportunity to learn alongside her same-age peers, to feel a sense of belonging, or to take pride in herself and her school. But in our district, she did.

*The following fall, Sunni started high school in our partner district. At a pep rally before the Crosstown rivalry game, her mother sent me a video of Sunni racing on a scooter with a partner before the entire student body. Long after the race had been won, Sunni and her partner were still working hard to get her—seated on the scooter—across the finish line. Her partner pushed, and Sunni held on, both of them determined. When the crowd of 1,400 students saw their determination, they began chanting in unison, "Sunni! Sunni! Sunni!" until she crossed the finish line. It was **belonging** at its best, and I still tear up whenever I watch that video.*

Four years later, Janice hand-delivered another announcement, this time announcing Sunni's high school graduation. In Sunni's own handwriting it read, "After high school, I will be working at Head Start Preschool." What a gift she will be to those young learners, and how lucky they are to have her guiding and inspiring them!

Students can't engage if they don't feel they belong. Even high achievers may disengage when they are uncomfortable or disconnected. Researchers Carol Goodenow and Kathleen Grady define *school belonging* as "the extent to which students feel personally accepted, respected, included, and supported by others in the school social environment."[1] For over a decade, we have observed, researched, written about, and championed the power of belonging. And its impact is clear: a strong sense of belonging supports improved academic achievement, attendance, comfort, positive relationships, deeper engagement, and effective classroom management. It offers a buffer against stress and severe mental health events. When students feel connected to their peers, teachers, and school, they are more likely to be involved in school and class activities, invest more thoroughly in their learning, and achieve at higher levels. Motivation increases, behavior issues decrease, and overall performance improves.[2] Belonging is not just important; it's an essential, fundamental need.

Put It Into Practice

Monitor Students' Sense of Belonging

To engage students with belonging, teachers need a strong "read" of how connected students feel. This requires intentional efforts to learn about each student's comfort level and to be continuously mindful of how belonging affects attendance, focus, instruction, learning, classroom climate, and overall school life. Even the best lesson may fall flat if a student is dealing with personal challenges such as a big fight with her best friend:

- Find or design an assessment tool. Many schools assess belonging through school climate or belonging surveys, often using student questionnaires or connectedness scales.[3] If your school does not do this, find more casual ways to check in on students' sense of belonging. Start early in the year, and revisit belonging status often (making sure to get administrative permission before using any surveys with students).

  Two helpful ways to get a sense of student belonging are to ask them to complete an anonymous survey and to invite their suggestions for improving a sense of belonging in the class. For the survey, ask students to rate statements (see examples below) from 1 to 4: *4-Most of the Time, 3-Often, 2-Sometimes, 1-Rarely.* (If your survey is only for your class, replace the word *school* with *class.*):

- I feel like I belong in this school.
- There is at least one adult at school who knows me well and understands me.
- I have trusting relationships with teachers.
- I have positive relationships with other students.
- I feel cared for in this school.
- I have friends to hang out with in and out of school.
- I feel that I am contributing to this school.
- I feel unwanted or excluded in this school.
- I don't have any close connections at this school.
- I don't feel very involved in school activities.
- I feel like I have to act a certain way that is not who I really am in order to be accepted by my friends and/or teachers.
- Be sure to make good use of what you hear from students. Pay attention to the trends in the responses. Then, invite students, working in pairs or small groups, to make suggestions about improving belonging. They can address these categories:
  - What individuals already do or could do to increase their own belonging
  - What students already do or could do to help each other belong
  - What the teacher already does or could do to help students increase belonging

Find ways to put students' ideas to work. (A student points out that the seating arrangements keep cliques together and lead to others feeling like outsiders. The teacher hears this, breaks up cliques, and mixes students more heterogeneously. Students make connections with peers they may have ignored before, and the student who gave the feedback tells the teacher that the problem has improved.) Identify specific actions that individuals, the group, and the teacher can take. Discuss how teachers and students can consistently put these into practice. Keep track of strategies you try, and pay attention to what works. Investigate underlying causes of disconnectedness (loneliness due to lack of friendships in the classroom or insecurity about ability to do well in the class), and watch for obstacles to belonging. Ask students for feedback about their sense of belonging in class or school and how it may have changed (and why).

Build a Culture of Belonging

If we want to use belonging to deepen engagement for our students, we must start by examining and refining (where needed) school and classroom culture. Students are most likely to thrive in an environment where everyone is dedicated to fostering a sense of belonging for themselves and for all members of the school community.[4] Actions such as these will help build a foundation for increased belonging:

- Consider these proven influences on belonging. Are they at work in your classroom? How can you tell? Ask students. Hold discussions or surveys where students give input about what factors help them (and others) belong. Ask them specifically if the attributes below exist in their classroom and, if so, what difference they make. But be open to hearing other factors that are not on this list. They can give impressions from other classrooms, too (without naming teachers).
  - An environment that is welcoming, respectful, caring, and safe (physically, socially, and emotionally)
  - Consistent, reliable, and trusting student-teacher relationships
  - Intentional and effective practices for supporting positive peer relationships
  - Authentic opportunities for students' involvement in their own learning and school life
  - Active recognition, value, and incorporation of each student's experiences and culture

- Regular practices that increase belonging for students' families
- Regular collaborative experiences that involve students working together in many different combinations to do meaningful tasks
- Make belonging a priority for professional development. Join with colleagues to learn best practices for boosting belonging for students and their families.
- Don't neglect to address belonging for all adults on staff. Just as belonging energizes engagement for students, it also makes adults more effective and engaged educators. A few ideas:
  - Just as you assess belonging status for students, survey staff a few times each year to get a picture of their sense of belonging. (It's a good idea to do the same for students' families.)
  - Create a sign that teachers can place outside their classroom door when they're teaching a lesson they believe would be valuable for others to observe. The sign should communicate: Feel free to stop in and watch my class, even for a few minutes.
  - Host staff recognition opportunities throughout the year at monthly staff meetings, board meetings, and in front of students in classrooms.
  - A few times a week, before students arrive, have adults gather in the hallway and make a line for a morning handshake with one another. The person at the head of the line shakes hands and says good morning to the next person and so on down the line. Result: Everyone touches base with each other to start the day.
  - Create opportunities for staff to sit with different colleagues at each meeting, giving them a chance to collaborate and get to know one another.

Share staff expertise by holding internal professional learning opportunities. Staff can choose from three to four topics to learn about from other staff members.

+ Join with colleagues to establish practices that nourish and sustain belonging schoolwide. We have been long-time champions of the powers of belonging in schools. This passion led us to write two books and give dozens of presentations on the topic. For more help with establishing culture and practices for belonging, see *The Successful Middle School: A Place to Belong and Become* and *We Belong: 50 Strategies to Create Community and Revolutionize Classroom Management.*[5]

+ Build and sustain a place where kids want to be. Belonging grows when teachers greet students by name, connect with each one daily (even briefly), laugh and listen together, give positive feedback, provide chances for students to contribute positively to the school or community, and share good news with families through phone calls, postcards, or emails. I (Patti) remember our staff doing a postcard "blitz" to make sure every student received a positive postcard within a two-week period. We had parents and caregivers in tears calling teachers saying it was the first time they'd ever received a positive note about their child.

Recognize Students in Multiple Ways

Recognizing students in multiple ways promotes a broad and inclusive definition of success, reinforcing the message that every student has strengths worth celebrating and a meaningful place in our school community.

At Laurie's junior high school—which operates under the middle school model—our staff is deeply committed to ensuring every student feels seen, heard, valued, and included. One way we foster this sense of belonging is through our regular Quarterly Student Recognition

Assemblies to celebrate students for high achievement or growth in five key areas: attendance, attitude, academics, athletics, and arts. A highlight of one end-of-year assembly was a performance by a student rock band, formed through friendships in their music class. With the support of their music teacher, who supervised after-school student-led practices, the group even recruited a paraprofessional–a professional musician in two bands–to join them. Their performance was such a hit that they were invited to play again at the 8th-grade celebration event for students and the community.

At Patti's school, they discovered a simple way to acknowledge students and encourage them to listen to the morning announcements read by a student over the intercom each day. The last daily announcement was, *And today's Student of the Day is… Come to the office to receive your prize.* Prizes were something simple like a pencil, a snack bar, etc. At the beginning of the year, every student's name was put into a large container; when new students enrolled, their names were added. It was a purely random selection with no criteria required. Once a student's name was pulled, it was discarded for the remainder of that year. It was amazing how excited students were to hear their name pulled. I remember overhearing an 8th grader brag that his name had been pulled three times, once each year.

Ensure an Adult Advocate for Every Student

It is critical that every student has at least one trusted adult at school. From young adolescents to those preparing for adulthood, having a caring, dependable adult is essential to fostering a sense of belonging.

When I (Laurie) am in the unfortunate position of holding a discipline hearing in the superintendent's office, I always ask the student involved who his or her most trusted adult on campus is. Too often, the student struggles to name even one person. Many of the students making poor choices in school (and in life) are those who feel isolated, lack supportive peers, and have no trusted adult they can confide in or turn to for guidance.

There are many ways to determine whether each student in your school, no matter its size or grade levels, has a trusted adult on campus. One simple and effective method is to create a brief survey using Google Forms or another platform. (Again, always obtain administrator approval before surveying students.) Using a dropdown menu, list every staff member in the school–teachers, paraprofessionals, administrators, secretaries, custodians, food service workers, safety personnel, and support staff–in alphabetical order. Then, ask three questions:

1. *Who is your primary trusted adult at school, the person you can go to when you need help?*
2. *Who would be your second choice?*
3. *Who would be your third choice?*

Have all students complete the survey. Then share with staff the names of any students who listed them for any of the three questions. (The order doesn't need to be shared.) This recognition not only affirms the impact those staff members are having but also strengthens their sense of purpose in continuing to build meaningful connections.

For students who listed no trusted adults, discuss the results at your next staff meeting. Ask for volunteers (from all staffing areas) to "adopt" a student (or several students) and intentionally work to form a positive, trusting relationship.

Patti used a variation on this at her school. A list of all student names was posted on the staff room walls. All adults in the building were to "star" students with whom they had an exceptionally strong relationship, knowing the student and perhaps even the family, quite well. Next, they put a "plus" by names of students with whom they had a positive but less deep relationship. Top students and difficult students got the most stars and plusses. Sadly, we found too many "invisible" students with no marks by their name. We divided those students up among adults who knew them and committed to fostering relationships with those students. We encouraged teachers to use a consistent greeting with the student's name, to make specific positive comments, and to ask for their help with a simple task. The goal was to make repeated positive interactions, because, over time, these small, regular connections will help students feel known, valued, and supported.

Help Students Find Their Places

Another key component of belonging for students is finding "their place," a group or community in which they feel accepted, valued, and part of something bigger than themselves. It's important that all students have a space outside the traditional classroom where they feel they fit and want to be (and are wanted). We need to consider whether each of our students has such a community and be ready to help those who do not find their ways to "their place."

When we (Laurie and my husband) dropped our daughter Emma off for her freshman year of college, the mix of immense pride and deep sadness was almost overwhelming. As her dad and I drove away—with both Emma and me in tears—I felt an immediate sense of comfort watching her join her new college soccer teammates. I knew she wouldn't be navigating her new world alone. Later that evening, when she called to tell us about the locker room chatter, team dinner, and hanging out with her teammates, my heart was at ease. She had already found her people. She belonged. No matter the age, we all want that feeling of belonging.

To better understand how connected students feel at school, you can expand the trusted adult survey shared above to include a few questions about involvement. In that same survey, add two more questions:

4. *What school activities are you involved in? Check all that apply to you.* (Provide students with a checkbox list that includes every sport, music program, performing arts program, club, or activity your school offers outside regular classes.)
5. *What are your out-of-school activities? List any groups, organizations, or other activities that you take part in regularly outside of school.*

If a student reports no involvement in either category, discreetly discuss those students at your next staff meeting. Ask for volunteers to reach out to those students, learn about their interests, and help connect them to an activity, club, or group where they can feel included and valued. All students deserve to have a place—and people—where they belong.

Offer Cross-Grade Opportunities for Belonging

I (Patti) once had a student tell me how excited he was to finally be in 7th grade. Since he was very athletic, I assumed it was because he would get to play on school sports teams. But he smiled and said, "No! It's because my friends from elementary school will be here!" His response was such a great reminder that belonging often stems from relationships and connection. When students have the chance to learn, work, and play together over time, their sense of belonging naturally deepens. Likewise, when they are able to stay with the same teacher for more than one year, it strengthens relationships and helps teachers truly know, understand, and advocate for their students.

There are several ways schools can structure programs to support these kinds of lasting relationships. And while some ideas have district-level implications to develop, they may trigger ideas for possibilities in your school:

+ Blend classrooms. When enrollment numbers don't neatly fit grade-level sections, consider creating blended classrooms with students from two grade levels. This is sometimes a common practice in elementary schools.

+ Move the teacher with the students to the next grade level (looping). Teachers can move up a grade level with their students. Patti taught 5th grade one year and moved with her class to 6th grade the next.

+ Build long-term advisory programs. At Phoenix High School in Oregon, students are placed in a multi-grade homeroom or advisory and keep the same advisor for all four years. Incoming 9th graders are welcomed and mentored by older students, creating a built-in support network and a strong sense of community. For great advice on advisory programs and practices, see *The Successful Middle School Advisory* by Todd Brist.[6]

+ Keep counseling assignments consistent. When Laurie taught high school, each student was assigned to a counselor who stayed with them for all four years, allowing for stronger, more personal connections.

+ Plan cross-grade activities. At a friend's elementary school, older students who struggled with reading practiced reading simple children's books and then were paired one-on-one with kindergarten or 1st-grade students to read aloud to their partner.

+ Structure multi-grade teams. At Patti's middle school, teams were multi-graded, combining language arts and social studies with the same core teachers for three years. Classes were blended by grade, curricula rotated to cover all content, and students stayed in the same advisory group with the same peers and advisor throughout middle school.

As a middle school principal (Patti), there was always something special about attending the Phoenix High School graduation and seeing students who had once roamed our middle school halls walk across the stage. The school had a unique tradition of allowing graduating seniors to honor an adult who had played a significant role in their education. Each senior was asked to identify an adult in the school district to introduce the student at graduation. The adults wore graduation robes and walked down the aisle with and were seated beside their student(s).

Some adults introduced multiple students, while others might introduce just one, such as a kindergarten teacher presenting a senior who had never forgotten that very first teacher. Personnel from all district schools and grade levels are included each year, from counselors and classroom teachers to principals, custodians, bus drivers, special education aides, and more. Adults are typically invited to share a sentence or two about the student.

I vividly remember a soccer coach introducing one of his star players, noting that while the student had been the team's top scorer, on graduation day he was making the biggest play of his life by becoming the first person in his family to graduate from high school.

This practice beautifully highlights the bonds that help students feel connected and reinforces the message that the district is a place where they belong.

CHAPTER 7

ENGAGE Students with Peer Interaction

When I (Laurie) began my career as a high school English teacher, my mom gave me a small, undeniably cheesy plaster bust of William Shakespeare. "Willie," as he came to be known, took a proud spot on my classroom shelf, overseeing his modern-day scholars. I often consulted him about a poem or had students share their thoughts with him, earning indulgent laughter and a few eye rolls from my classes.

My 12th-grade AP Literature class, however, adored Willie. They'd bring him to their discussion groups or keep him close during stressful essays. One student even swore his presence on her desk earned her a top score.

After winter break one year, on the day of a major exam, the TV suddenly flicked on as I entered the classroom. To my shock, there was Willie—on screen, missing from his shelf—starring in a video documenting his "kidnapping" and "international travels" over the break. The ransom demand? Postpone the day's scheduled exam, and let them use the period to study.

I was torn between annoyance and admiration, but creativity won. I granted their request, and, after making me turn around so I could not *see who had Willie in captivity (it was Sam, and I know it!), Willie reappeared. What followed was the most engaged and collaborative study session I've ever witnessed. Students formed groups, moved freely, and discussed passionately. Willie made his rounds with me, observing a community of learners at their best.*

I don't remember what that exam even covered, but I'll never forget those students, their camaraderie, or their love of learning. Willie still sits on a shelf in my office today, and every time I see him, I smile.

While simply staying awake in class isn't the ultimate goal, it's a necessary first step toward engagement and, ultimately, learning. Peer interaction is a powerful way to build that engagement. With just one teacher in the room, peer collaboration greatly expands learning opportunities because students can learn from one another in addition to learning independently and from the teacher. When students work together, they share ideas, give feedback, teach one another, and check for understanding, turning every moment into a chance to strengthen and extend learning. Offer many rich opportunities for students to interact in diverse situations and groupings every day. Intentionally form these heterogeneous groups so students can connect with peers beyond their usual circles.

Research on brain-compatible learning has taught us that brains are social; they work and learn and remember better when working with other brains.[1] Other research shows that positive peer contacts and influences can serve as powerful forces for student learning and well-being. In the presence of safe and trusting relationships, peers can offer one another social and emotional support; opportunities to learn prosocial behavior; models for motivation, work habits, and self-management; practice in empathy, responsibility, problem-solving, and conflict resolution; academic challenge and risk-taking; and greater self-awareness and confidence.[2]

The more positive and successful interactions students have with one another, the stronger and more lasting these benefits become, building on each experience over time.

Put It Into Practice

Promote simple peer interactions

Before students can truly cooperate and collaborate, they need to feel comfortable interacting in non-threatening ways. The following activities across different social groups combine interaction, movement, and critical thinking and promote peer interaction through high engagement, teamwork, and skill-building:

> Before students can truly cooperate and collaborate, they need to feel comfortable interacting in non-threatening ways.

- **Group Discussions:** Help students build communication, critical thinking, and confidence by sharing and listening to ideas. Teachers guide (not dominate) conversations, keeping them focused, respectful, and inclusive. A good resource for teachers of all grade-levels and subjects is Mathew Kay's book *Promoting Deeper Discussions: A Teacher's Guide to Crafting Great Questions*.[3]
- **Four Corners:** Ask a question with four answer choices, and have students move to the corner (with an option posted on the wall) that matches their answer. Once there, they discuss why they chose it and prepare to defend their thinking. This strategy works for opinions, vocabulary, reviewing content, or solving math problems. It helps students think critically, listen

to different perspectives, and discuss respectfully. In another variation, an 8th-grade English teacher might label each corner with a poster showing two sentences containing some type of a clause or a mixture of types of clauses (noun, adverb, or adjective). Only one poster has adverb clauses. Students are asked, *Which of the displayed sentences contain adverb clauses?* For a more open-ended prompt, a teacher might ask: *Which invention has had the greatest impact: vaccines, the lightbulb, the wheel, or the smartphone?* Students choose a corner and build arguments to support their choice.

+ **Friendly Competition:** In small teams, students answer review questions for points. Include challenges that promote teamwork, like quick drawings or acting out concepts.

+ **Gallery Walks:** Post topic-related items around the room (questions, images, quotes). Students walk the "gallery" in pairs or small groups, discuss each item, and record insights before sharing with the class. They can assign one student to be the "recorder" who keeps notes. When sharing insights, student groups might project these on a display screen or write out phrases on a paper to tape on the wall near each item.

+ **Storytelling:** Students retell or create stories related to what they've learned. Try a round-robin version where each student adds to the story. After studying the concept and cycle of metamorphosis in animals, one group of 3rd graders decided to tell a story about a tadpole. They gave the creature a name and passed the story along, each one adding a sentence or an event to show their understanding of the cycle. Of course, when finished, they started another story with a caterpillar as the main character.

+ **Team Creations:** In small groups, use limited materials (like straws and tape) to build the tallest self-supporting structure in fifteen minutes. Add a "silent collaboration" rule for extra challenge.

- **Speed Dating:** Students form two circles, one inside the other, with partners facing each other to discuss open-ended questions. Give each student 30–90 seconds to answer a question. Then rotate to a new partner and new question. This is ideal for review and critical thinking (and to add movement).

- **Think-Pair-Share:** Present students with a written question or prompt, and give them a few minutes to THINK and jot down ideas. Then PAIR them up to share their responses and explain their reasoning. Each pair chooses the most persuasive or interesting ideas. Bring the class back together and have many (or all) pairs SHARE their selected responses and the thinking behind them. Encourage both partners to contribute, and allow time for a brief whole-class discussion to deepen understanding.

- **10-2-2 Chunk and Chew:** This method focuses on teachers breaking a topic into smaller chunks, teaching one of those at a time, and stopping to give students time to "chew" on what they learned before moving on to more parts of the topic. Teach something for ten minutes. Students meet in pairs for two minutes to engage on what was taught (provide a prompt, format, activity, or structure for this). Finally, students process the ideas individually for themselves for two minutes, through note-taking, completing a graphic organizer, or responding to prompts in a guided notebook. Then the teacher goes on to the next "chunk."

Arrange Cross-Grade or Cross-School Interactions

While we generally think of peer interaction as occurring within a classroom, look for opportunities to create interactions that cross grades or even schools.

When Patti taught 6th grade, students dissected squid as part of a unit on oceanography. To prepare, the 8th-grade science teacher trained his students to become "squid squad" experts. When it was time for the dissection, a squid squad joined us to teach and guide the process. They helped each team of students open the squid, identify body parts, find the ink sac, and even use the ink to write their names with the squid's pen. We ended the activity by frying squid rings for a calamari feast. It was hands-on, engaging, and memorable learning at its best.

In Laurie's district, after 5th graders finish studying Colonial America and 8th graders finish studying Lewis and Clark, the two groups come together to share the personal journals they've kept during their studies. Each student has written from the perspective of someone living in that time, and sharing their work with peers outside their class creates a powerful, authentic learning experience.

Understand the True Meaning of Collaboration

Students working together is valuable but only when there is a clear purpose with defined goals and strong guidance. Not all group work is truly collaborative; some is merely cooperative. If students simply divide tasks and work separately, or if some members carry the load for others, that's cooperation—not collaboration. They are working together but not joining in the full responsibility of each member for the outcomes. Real collaboration means all members contribute, rely on one another's thinking, and share responsibility for their own work **and** for the final product. So while a group creating a slideshow may divide tasks, each student still helps find resources, supports others' work, and takes equal ownership of the final presentation. This reminds me of a lesson I (Patti) learned back in 4th grade. My group of three was assigned a class presentation on a topic. We decided each of us would write our own report and then present them together. Unfortunately, we never compared our work. When presentation day came, the first person read her report—word for word from the encyclopedia. The second person did the exact same thing. By the time it was my turn, I told the teacher mine was identical, but she insisted I read it anyway to our thoroughly bored classmates. Lesson learned: when you're assigned group work, actually *work together*, not separately—collaborate. (And maybe don't copy straight from the encyclopedia either!)

- Help students understand collaboration. Explain that it is built on *positive interdependence*, the idea that every group member is responsible for the individual part but is also essential to achieving the team's goal, and each person's contribution is equally valuable. According to Shelly Berman, who studies the processes by which children develop social responsibility, this kind of structure fosters genuine connection.[4] When students in heterogeneous groups rely on one another to succeed, they develop stronger bonds and a deeper sense of belonging, and they demonstrate more kindness and prosocial behavior.

  In fact, this *positive interdependence*, found at the heart of true collaboration, is one of the most effective ways to reduce bias and prejudice. It encourages students to reconsider assumptions about others, see their peers in new ways, and grow in acceptance and empathy.[5] This is the powerful learning that engages students not just cognitively but also socially, emotionally, and behaviorally.

- Intentionally plan collaboration with clear structure and purposeful instructional design. Effective collaboration doesn't happen by chance; it requires thoughtful preparation and instruction around how students will work together and why.

Base planning on these characteristics of collaboration:

- **Basic success requirement:** The task can only be accomplished by working together and depending on one another's strengths. If one person's main role is to provide visual images for a project, other group members will depend on that member's capabilities and reliability to do the task. The same is true for the person who will write the first draft of informational captions. All students may review and contribute to these later, but they depend on the original author to do the job well.
- **Personal accountability:** Every member is responsible for individual learning and for completing that portion of the work fully and well.
- **Group accountability:** Each person shares responsibility for the group's overall success and for helping every other member succeed.
- **Group well-being:** All members ensure that everyone feels respected, supported, and comfortable within the group.
- **Supporting each other:** Members use clear communication, problem-solving, and conflict-resolution skills to work through challenges.
- **Valuing the process:** The way students work and learn together matters just as much as the final product or outcome.

Plan Interactions that Foster Interdependence

The key to highly engaging peer interactions is interdependence: students working, discussing, creating, and planning together in a truly collaborative manner, where every member is dependent on every other member to fully participate, to come through with their specified contribution, to take part in putting parts together, and to evaluate and refine the final phases. There are many activities that foster this true collaboration:

+ Pair students for a close-reading activity using purposeful annotations. Choose a short, meaningful passage rich in language or ideas, and form pairs that balance readiness and perspectives. Clearly define the reading goal—such as analyzing tone, finding evidence, or interpreting meaning. Establish a consistent annotation system (underlining key ideas, circling unfamiliar words, noting questions or reactions). After reading, partners compare notes, discuss differences, and ask critical questions while the teacher circulates to guide thinking and address confusion. The activity can end with a class discussion, an annotated-text gallery, or a brief reflection. In true collaboration, both students contribute equally, listen to each other, make joint decisions about their final product, and can explain their individual contributions as well as the value of the outcome. This method works well with textbook passages, readings, or articles in any subject.

+ Use simulations. Give each team a set amount of classroom "money" (for example, $10,000) to invest. Students research companies and explain why their picks would be smart investments. After group discussion, the team decides together how to allocate their funds. Over the next few weeks, they track their portfolio using real-time stock data and decide when to buy, sell, or hold based on market trends or news. At the end, teams calculate gains or losses and reflect on what influenced their choices, what strategies worked, and what they would change. A final class discussion connects their experience to real-world economics. To ensure true interdependence, all students participate in research, all investment decisions are made by consensus, and all team members share responsibility for the group's work, reflection, and application of ideas.

+ Jigsaw frequently. The jigsaw method of collaborative learning has been used for years in many settings. It has been shown to boost understanding, achievement, student interdependence, and peer relationships.[6] Here's how it works.

Before you begin: Place students in small, heterogeneous "home groups." Each student in each group receives one part of a larger topic to learn in depth and become an "expert."

Step 1: Expert Groups
Students join others who are studying the same section of material. Together, they read or watch the content, identify main ideas, discuss its importance, and decide how it connects to the larger topic. They plan how to teach their part to their home groups and record key points to share.

Step 2: Home Groups
Students rejoin their home groups. Each "expert" teaches the assigned section, explaining main ideas and insights. Teammates take notes, ask questions, and clarify understanding of each part as experts explain. By the end, everyone should understand the complete topic—all pieces of the puzzle. Everyone is given a copy of the full material with all the parts or topics.

Step 3: Reflection or Assessment
Still in home groups, students reflect on or take part in a formative assessment covering all of the content to ensure full understanding by all students. This may take the form of a discussion, group project, or quiz.

Optional Step 4: Expert Group Reflection
Back in expert groups, students discuss how their section fit and contributed to the overall meaning, how it connected to the other parts, and why it was important to the whole.

Make Time for Students to Socialize

Positive peer influence extends far beyond academics, shaping how students make choices about friends, social media, risk-taking, and life in general. Simply having time to talk with one another during classes also builds stronger relationships and provides valuable mental breaks. For many children and adolescents, the heavy obsession with screen time and online interaction limits their capacities to navigate face-to-face interactions. Because of this, students often experience anxiety and discomfort when they have to work with others in-person instead of through digital apps or carefully-curated online media platforms. The need for students to experience face-to-face interactions and learn to live and work together off-screen needs high-priority attention in classrooms.

Wise teachers and schools intentionally schedule time for these connections. Planned in-class time for social interaction is especially important in upper grades where students no longer have recess.[7] In addition to saving time to "just talk to each other," offer multiple situations for face-to-face interactions that are not specific to a content learning goal: playing board games, interviewing one another about personal interests, or (in pairs or small groups) sharing answers to (appropriate) Would you rather? Questions.

When we talk about student engagement through peer interactions, a common concern is that when students work together without direct adult supervision they will be talking more about weekend plans or last night's social media posts than algebra or the Industrial Revolution. I (Laurie) have led many staff meetings and professional learning sessions over the last few decades, and, honestly, I can't think of one without someone sharing an "off-task" or personal comment, and that's OK with me. High level engagement sometimes involves getting off task.

During my first year as a superintendent, I witnessed a powerful example of this when observing a choir class: The kids were restless and clearly tuning out. The teacher was trying to regain control, and I was debating whether to slip out so I wouldn't make things worse. Then the teacher called out, "Everyone stop! You have sixty seconds to talk about anything you want that's not related to this class. Go!" A minute later, he shouted, "Stop! OK, we're on line three–ready?" And just like that, the singing started and carried beautifully through the remainder of the period. It was the smartest use of 60 seconds I think I've witnessed. He had traded one minute for twenty solid minutes of focus.

An elementary teacher colleague shared this story with us: One summer the primary teachers at my school attended a workshop that focused on using math discourse to have students talk, write, and think together about mathematics. Students weren't asked to just give an answer; they were asked to share their thinking on how they came up with an answer, why it works, and how different strategies can result in the same answer. This caused us to slow down our math instruction, and instead of just showing my 2nd graders what to do in order to solve the problem, I focused on the "Why?" behind the process.

For example, when adding two-digit numbers I asked students to work in pairs to add 34 plus 28 and be ready to explain how they figured out the answer. One group shared, "We stacked them and added 4 plus 8 is 12, so we put down 2 and carried the 1, because 12 has one ten and two ones so we move the ten over. Our answer is 62."

Another group explained, "We added 30 and 20 first to get 50, then 4 and 8 to get 12. So, 50 plus 12 is 62." Soon, the room would be buzzing with conversation as students compared strategies, drew number models, and helped each other see why the methods worked. By the end of class, students weren't just solving problems, they were explaining, questioning, and connecting ideas.

Over time, I saw a real change in my classroom. My students stopped just memorizing steps and began truly understanding how math works. They were excited to work together, finding different ways to solve problems and sharing their thinking with their classmates.

CHAPTER 8

ENGAGE Students with Compelling Content

When I (Patti) first became an assistant principal, my school district faced a significant budget shortfall that led to teacher layoffs. In some cases, when a position was eliminated, staff with greater seniority were reassigned to positions for which they were certified but not highly qualified. For example, elementary counselors with English certifications were sometimes moved to teach middle school English language arts.

One teacher from a downsizing elementary school had a teaching certificate allowing her to teach nearly every subject in grades K–8 and was reassigned to teach math at my middle school. Previously, she had been a successful 5th-grade teacher, but she was now assigned 6th- and 7th-grade math.

As the year progressed, classroom management became a major challenge; students were frequently off task, disruptive, and disrespectful, particularly in 7th grade. Initially, we thought the difficulty stemmed from her working with older students, but through observations and conversations, we realized the core issue was her limited understanding of the underlying math concepts beyond basic computation. She had assumed that because students could perform arithmetic, they fully understood foundational *concepts such as place value and number sense, which are essential for more advanced math.*

When she attempted to teach fractions, decimals, introductory algebra, and basic geometry, students became confused. They asked questions she couldn't answer, and classroom chaos ensued.

Although she was "certified" to teach middle school math, it was clear that she lacked a deep understanding of the concepts and mathematical language necessary to provide students with the foundation they needed for success in higher-level courses.

Content is the foundation of education. Building strong relationships, a positive classroom culture, and connected learning communities is critical, but these efforts must work alongside high-quality content taught effectively by well-trained teachers. Neither can replace the other; both are essential.

Content is far more than textbooks or curriculum guides for a specific subject. It encompasses the knowledge, skills, concepts, processes, attitudes, and values students learn in a subject. Most content comes from school-approved materials, but teachers also shape, adapt, and add to it. When students connect with content, they are more likely to engage with the entire learning experience, participating fully. When students are not drawn to the content in class, they miss out on the benefits of powerful learning.

Put It Into Practice

Master Your Content

In order to teach students (required) content that grabs their interest and connects with something that leads to their investment in learning it, a teacher must first have a thorough knowledge of the content to be taught and know how to teach it. These actions will contribute to your knowledge and skill with your content:

- Know your content well. At a minimum, effectively teaching your subject requires strong content knowledge. You must have a thorough and flexible understanding of the foundational concepts within your subject area. Incomplete or vague knowledge from teachers will interfere with offering students the content and relevance that sparks and expands their engagement.
- Follow the guidelines of your curriculum:
  - Know and understand your content standards and expected outcomes at your grade level, as well as the ones that come before and after them. This puts the expectations in a context of what and how students learned before and what their learning in your class prepares them for later. Students get the satisfaction of using previous knowledge to learn next-level concepts and catch a glimpse of what they'll be able to do next!
  - As discussed in Chapter 4, follow your school's pacing guide or scope and sequence to ensure appropriate progression through the standards. Skilled teachers with strong content expertise can make slight strategic adjustments to better support learning, as long as they return to the intended pace and progression. However, teachers who are still developing this expertise should rely more closely on the pacing guide to avoid creating gaps or disrupting the learning sequence. When used wisely, a pacing guide can be both a roadmap and a tool for informed professional judgment.
- Seek professional development that strengthens your content knowledge, improves your teaching practices, and fosters student engagement. Ask a colleague for help when teaching new material. Teaching can sometimes feel isolating, so whenever possible, visit other classrooms. Observe skilled colleagues (both in and out of your subject area) to learn valuable strategies and ideas to adapt to your own teaching. Participate in state

and national organizations dedicated to your content area; subscribe and read professional journals in your field. Seek online tutorials or participate in online forums and professional learning networks on topics related to what you teach. Take courses at local colleges to get special training or an advanced degree in your content area.

+ Be prepared to present your content in multiple ways. To meet needs of individual students, break complex topics into logical, sequential steps so students can follow and build understanding. Even if it's your 23rd year teaching the concept, it's probably the student's first year learning about it. Not only is this beneficial to students, but it also helps teachers engage deeply with the concepts and master their content.

+ Predict areas where students might struggle. Prepare explanations, examples, or analogies ahead of time to help them better understand. We cannot overemphasize the value of anticipating where students might struggle with content. Doing this helps you notice how students in the past have received the content and leads you to investigate the content closely to understand what about it might be problematic for students.

+ Be aware of students' fears about your class content or learning in general. Work to minimize those fears. Some arrive anxious about math, writing, science, or other subjects, fearing failure or judgment. Address this early by acknowledging their concerns and reassuring them that you understand and will help them succeed despite their fears. Share your own journey in mastering this content, as a teacher or as a student yourself. Tell how you came to understand certain concepts, what strategies helped you, and how you overcame the anxiety. Tell students what excites you about the content. Explaining this broadens your own connection and competence with the content and can help inspire their confidence.

Ensure that Content Inspires and Connects with Students

Learning the content must remain a top priority in every class. This doesn't mean there's no room for fun, storytelling, addressing social needs, celebrating success, or taking quick breaks. But since content is at the heart of classroom learning, it must be presented in ways that trigger students' curiosity, interest, and investment. Not all required content will naturally appeal to everyone. So it takes high-quality instruction to make any content relevant, intriguing, and applicable to students' experiences and goals. That's engagement! These actions will help you offer content in ways that engage students:

> But since content is at the heart of classroom learning, it must be presented in ways that trigger students' curiosity, interest, and investment.

+ Use diverse content sources. Don't rely solely on traditional or familiar materials. In addition to your school's approved curriculum, explore a variety of trustworthy information sources to enrich instruction. A few notes of caution:
  - Always make sure any supplementary materials align with learning standards and are age-appropriate (and follow your school's guidelines for using supplemental materials).
  - If you use digital tools requiring student data (names or identification numbers), get administrative approval first to protect privacy and comply with school policies.
  - Read federal laws (FERPA and COPPA) about protecting children's rights and privacy. In light of the explosion of generative AI, online grading, assessment, feedback, and sharing, all classroom teachers must be aware of these.

- Design learning with students' perspectives in mind. Plan lessons and assignments around how students best understand and engage with content. Connect topics to real-world issues and their own lives, interests, and experiences. Consider what will spark their curiosity and show why the material matters. For example, connect study of weather in science to examples of weather patterns, features, and changes to weather they have experienced in their area or seen in current events. Identify inventions created during the Industrial Revolution and show students how these have influenced or led to today's gadgets and tools. Connect a short story about a kid moving frequently to new schools (e.g., "The Circuit" by F. Jimenez) to their own experiences of starting school for the first time or changing schools.

- Present interactive content. As often as possible, use resources where students actively participate in exploring and learning the content. Find content sources that lend themselves to situations where students question, interview, collaborate, find and follow clues, follow steps, or demonstrate as they learn. Hands-on and minds-on learning deepens comprehension and keeps students engaged.

- Offer varied and flexible learning options when possible. For complex or challenging content, provide different versions or choices for assignments, projects, group work, presentations, and assessments. Options let students show learning in ways that fit their strengths, interests, and skills, making content more accessible and meaningful. Two teachers assign 9th graders to compare and contrast two short stories with similar themes. One gives a prepared template with columns labeled "similar" and "different" and subtitles such as setting, characters, conflict, theme, and author viewpoint. The other offers a selection of short stories and informational essays on related topics, suggesting comparison categories but inviting students to add their own. This teacher also offers varied presentation options such as slide shows, paired speeches, diagrams, dramas, or posters and welcomes student suggestions for alternatives.

- Develop student experts by giving them structures, roles, and responsibilities that promote active learning and self-awareness. Set clear guidelines (ideally co-created with students) for setting learning goals, planning how to reach them, finding resources, managing time, monitoring progress, and evaluating outcomes. Encourage collaboration in shaping classroom protocols, solving problems independently, and taking responsibility for assignments. While teachers have traditionally driven engagement, students learn more deeply when they take ownership. Increase student agency by allowing choice within standards, such as selecting topics, resources, or learning approaches that align with goals and expectations.

- Work to minimize boredom in content. We know. This can be really challenging with some students. Some topics may seem dull to students (or maybe even to the teacher), but every subject can be made engaging. Present material in creative, relatable ways that connect to students' interests and experiences. Stay alert for signs of disengagement like zoning out or fidgeting, and adjust your approach to reengage them through movement, discussion, or new learning formats. See Chapter 9 for many ways to infuse life into learning experiences and keep students engaged cognitively, physically, and emotionally.

- Give all content the challenge test. Keep material neither too easy nor too hard, just enough to stretch thinking and skills. The right level of challenge builds persistence, curiosity, and a sense of achievement, all key to engagement. Focus on big ideas with broad applications (change, cause and effect, power, struggle). Have students find patterns and trends, and use materials that include abstract as well as concrete concepts. Add decisions to make or problems to solve, asking students to explain the content's relevance. Incorporate multiple perspectives on events, arguments, or claims, and discuss ethical or moral dilemmas found in stories or real situations.

Connect Content to Prior Knowledge

Prior knowledge is not just facts or problem-solving skills but also the collection of experiences and understanding a student brings to learning. It includes how a student understands and applies knowledge, meaning two students may know the same information but interpret or use it differently. One of the most effective ways to engage students with new material is to connect it to what they already know. Doing so increases both engagement and long-term understanding of the new content.[1] These actions will help connect new content to students' prior knowledge:

- Find out what students already know. Before teaching new content, use formal or informal assessments to discover what students understand and where there might be knowledge gaps. This helps you connect new material to what they know and plan targeted support:
  - Discuss the new topic, and observe how students respond.
  - Design and administer a diagnostic pre-test on the unit content and skills. Invite students to answer the questions to which they think they know the answers, and leave the others blank. (In many cases, you can use the posttest as the pretest, saving time and ensuring you pre-assess what you will actually post-assess.)
  - Have students show what they know using a list, mind map, diagram, drawing, or demonstration.

- Use short scavenger hunts to build understanding of new ideas or vocabulary. (Find something that shows the meaning of *formidable*. Find something that demonstrates the concept of *form and function*, and use it to explain the connection between the two.)

- Once you are clear on what students know, build on that prior knowledge by incorporating it into a lesson that uses it to learn new knowledge. After checking students' previous knowledge about ratios and equivalent ratios (a 6th-grade standard) and reviewing this until he is satisfied students are able to use these concepts fluently, a 7th-grade math teacher introduces the concept of a proportional relationship as two numbers (or variables) that are the same ratios. Students work in pairs to examine several sets of numbers or variables, checking to see if they are proportional (4/20 is the same ratio as 5/25). In a geography lesson, a teacher finds that many students are not familiar with the concept of elevation or how it is measured, so the teacher must establish some prior knowledge by teaching them about elevation (using diagrams or pictures and having students measure the elevation of components of the classroom). Then students are ready to apply this knowledge to read the key and scale and find information on elevation maps—and to make an elevation map after doing some measurements in their school yard. (See Chapter 3 for more about transferring prior knowledge to new contexts.)

- Respect that students come to your classroom with different levels and types of prior knowledge. Some may not recall anything related to the new topic, and that's OK. Avoid using previous knowledge (or lack thereof) in ways that could embarrass anyone. And know that connections will often develop naturally as learning progresses.

Show Enthusiasm About the Content

Teacher enthusiasm is the positive attitude, along with the energy and passion shown for a subject, teaching it, and supporting students as they learn. It's expressed through voice, facial expressions, gestures, movement, and student interactions. It demonstrates the excitement, approval, and encouragement that build team spirit. Students know if we're enthusiastic about what we're teaching. There is no hiding a lack of enthusiasm, and once it's on display, it's difficult to keep it from spreading.

Research shows teacher enthusiasm, especially in combination with teacher confidence, has a positive impact on student engagement, achievement, focus, motivation, recall, and persistence.[2] Students learn better, and the teacher's passion adds activity, warmth, and fun to the classroom. Plus, it is contagious (as is lack of enthusiasm).

When I (Laurie) was a second-year teacher, I learned a hard lesson. While teaching direct and indirect objects and predicate adjectives and nominatives to my advanced 10th-grade English class, I momentarily mixed up which functioned as which and wrote a sentence on the board that didn't come out the way I intended. The way I arranged the words (meant to illustrate how a direct object, an indirect object, a predicate adjective, or a predicate nominative functions in a sentence) ended up creating a completely different meaning than the grammatical point I was trying to model.

The teenage students erupted in laughter because the sentence, as written, could easily be interpreted as inappropriate. They could see that I had made a content knowledge mistake, that the word order was accidental rather than deliberate, but they still couldn't help laughing at the result.

I panicked and left the room to ask my colleague Daphne to take over. For the remainder of the year, I spent my lunch periods with her, studying grammar until it became one of my strengths. But that moment—standing in front of bright students without full confidence in my content—was almost enough to break me.

CHAPTER 9

ENGAGE Students with Active Learning Experiences

When my (Laurie's) daughter Emma was in 4th grade (she's now a college graduate), our family moved from Georgia to Montana, knowing no one. We quickly fell in love with northwest Montana and all it offered, but what left the biggest impression on me was how deeply Emma's school field trips and hands-on learning experiences shaped her and her education.

Field trips here were unlike anything I'd seen before. Over the years, Emma's classes went ice fishing, downhill and cross-country skiing, hiking to alpine lakes, camping to and from the Oregon coast and surfing in the Pacific, exploring Glacier National Park, and even experiencing a five-day snow science field trip to a backcountry lodge with summit hikes, backcountry skiing, and avalanche training. Each experience connected learning to the world around her.

When Emma was in 8th grade, her class took a multi-day history trip across Montana, and she tells about that experience:

"When I was in 8th grade, our class traveled across Montana to learn about the State's history. At the end of the trip, we created a travel brochure and memory booklet to show what we'd learned. We weren't given step-by-step directions. We were given a few learning objectives, and the rest was up to us. At first, that was intimidating, but it ended up being one of the most valuable learning experiences I've had.

It taught me to think independently, be creative, and take ownership of my work. I still remember that trip far more clearly than anything I learned from a textbook, and I still have those projects today. It showed me how powerful hands-on, real-world learning can be and how much we gain when we truly connect with the place where we live. In thinking back, I realize how important learning through new experiences is to a student's overall education. Wherever students are, they need to experience their community, what makes the local area special, and how their environment impacts them and others."

Hands-on, real-world experiences are essential because they connect content and concepts to practice, deepen understanding, and develop critical life skills (academic, personal, social, and emotional). Learning through experience prioritizes active engagement over passively receiving information. Students spend less time memorizing, sitting, and listening (though both memorizing and listening have importance for student success) and more time **doing and experiencing**. When students actively do the work (active minds and bodies), they are invested in learning. "Doing and experiencing" are not entirely about moving around. Yes, students of all ages need lots of movement. But *active learning experiences* are those in which students are actively involved and invested. This includes such activities as discussing, grappling with a new idea, creating (including "quiet creating" like writing, hypothesizing, imagining), decision making, guided group problem-solving, reflection, and many other experiences that don't involve a lot of muscle movement (other than the mouth and brain, that is). All of these lead to real engagement and deeper understanding.[1]

According to researchers Renate and Geoffrey Caine, authors of books on the principles of brain-based learning, much has been discovered about the way the brain learns. Students' involvement in their learning by doing and experiencing is crucial to learning that lasts. A few of these principles are:

1. "Learning engages the entire physiology . . . Anything that affects our physiological functioning affects our capacity to learn."[2] *Physiology* is the whole of all of the body's workings. Students learn better when teachers understand and fit learning activities to students' development and needs for movement, satisfaction, social interaction, emotional and physical stability, and safety.

2. "The brain understands and remembers best when facts and skills are embedded in natural spatial experiences."[3] Success depends on making use of many senses and immersing the learner in a multitude of complex and interactive experiences.

3. "The search for meaning is innate."[4] Students need a rich learning environment that addresses the need for meaning (connection, vibrancy, finding acceptance, understanding how we fit and matter in the world) and that satisfies the brain's enormous curiosity and hunger for novelty, discovery, and challenge.

Put It Into Practice

Capture Students' Attention

Dynamic, active lessons and engaging learning activities are essential to pique students' curiosity and catch (and sustain) their attention. Consider how deeply students are engaged in games and apps on their phones and other devices (experiences that grab their interest, demand quick thinking and decision-making, introduce novelty and surprises, and appeal through sound, color, and action). We've learned that a primary draw of these games and apps is their effects on brain chemistry, triggering the release of dopamine and creating a moderate sense of well-being, a kind of "high." (For more about this dopamine addiction and its effects on attention and learning, see Anna Lembke's *Dopamine Nation*, Jonathan Haidt's *The Anxious Generation*, and Jean Twenge's *iGen: Why Today's Super-Connected Kids Are Growing Up Less Rebellious, More Tolerant, Less Happy—and Completely Unprepared for Adulthood—and What That Means for the Rest of Us*.)[5]

Not every school lesson can or should replicate a video game or social media challenge. Still, students are most engaged when lessons include variety, novelty, movement, challenge, social interaction, technology, real-world relevance, and opportunities for lively involvement. We need to find ways to craft learning experiences that spark and sustain similar levels of engagement. Infuse into your instruction activities that release positive doses of dopamine for students. They can discover what makes something work, follow their curiosity to crack a content mystery, depict a concept or process with dance, join in a scavenger hunt, or solve a riddle or puzzle:

- Grab students' attention at the start of the lesson. Socrates said that all thinking begins with wonder. How might we create a sense of wonder and curiosity as we begin the day's learning? Create captivating hooks that make students look up and tune in. Use an intriguing question, a fascinating quote, a surprise announcement, a clever mime or monologue, a personal anecdote, a bizarre fact, an unusual statistic, a funny costume, an unexpected visitor in disguise (ask a colleague to help), five clues to a mystery, a riddle or puzzle, a joke, cartoon, or meme. Engagement isn't simply entertainment; it's anything that draws students in and keeps them involved. That said, there are countless ways to launch a lesson. The key is making sure your hook connects directly to your academic content and learning goals.

Once you have students' attention, you can smoothly transition into the purpose of the lesson.

You may be thinking, "I don't have time to build wonder and engagement into every lesson; we need to get right to work." And yes, it can take extra time. But the beginning of every lesson should have some type of hook, even if very brief. It's worth it. Wonder, novelty, and engagement are essential for learning. If you don't capture students' attention early, their learning is more fragile, and you'll likely spend even more time later reteaching or trying to increase their involvement.

+ Hang on to attention after the hook. Be ready with a range of activities and experiences that fit your curriculum and goals. We want students personally invested, even passionate, about learning. Use flexible, adaptable instructional strategies that capture attention, and gather ideas from colleagues, blogs, books, articles, and students themselves. When activities connect to students' lives and spark creativity and critical thinking, they're less likely to become bored or disruptive and more likely to persist and remember the experience. This keeps students engaged throughout the lesson. Some effective strategies include gallery walks, fishbowl discussions, virtual tours, student TED talks, mock trials, digital or physical scavenger hunts, interviews, Socratic seminars, concept maps, and jigsaw activities.

Involve Students in Learning by DOING

Plan for active learning. Make yourself a checklist of indicators that shows you've planned learning experiences that, indeed, will lead to active engagement. Include such questions for yourself as: *In this week's lessons, where are students negotiating their responses to content questions with others? Where are they being asked to interact with more than one idea at a time? Where are they revising their efforts in light of what they've learned in the first few steps of something? Where have they broken concepts down into their component pieces (analysis)? Where have they brought two or more things together to form something new (synthesis)? Where have they transferred something they learned earlier in this class to a new context? Where have they discovered that they could use different strategies to solve the same problem?* Expose students to lessons and assignments that:

- Reinforce that the process of "doing" is often as, or even more, valuable than the final outcome. Students build skills, deepen understanding, and learn new concepts by planning, finding and analyzing resources, pursuing answers, explaining their thinking, correcting mistakes, trying new strategies, discussing ideas, and teaching others. Every part of this process contributes to meaningful learning. (For more on meaningful learning, see Chapter 12.) Remind students of the value of these steps, which are often overlooked when the focus is only on getting the right answer.

- Use multiple instructional strategies, assignments, assessments, and materials, and offer alternative ways to explore the same concept when needed. A unit on tornado patterns might begin with a video, a visit to a weather center, or a simulated trip inside a volcano. When sharing the meaning of a novel, students can diagram the plot, role-play key events with peers, or perform dramatic readings with brief explanations that highlight the book's central message.

- Offer many opportunities within the standards for students to lead their own learning and to make meaningful choices and decisions about what and how they learn and to show what they learn.

- Encourage students to express and share their plans, opinions, ideas, questions, responses, and reflections.

- Include breaks for students' brains and bodies. Use breaks for needed movement, socializing, relaxation, creativity, and collaboration. Take a two-minute rest and relax break: relax, take deep breaths, and listen to calming music. Do a minute of silent jumping jacks, a yoga pose, body stretches, or a two-minute dance-off to (approved) music chosen by students. Try a freeze dance (same rules as musical chairs; stop the music, anyone not frozen leaves the floor.)

Students need experiences that will engage them meaningfully; this will happen best with an activity that is tied to specific learning goals and content that is important for students to learn. Below are some sample active learning experiences you might try, adapt, or expand with your students. Most can involve peer collaboration. (See more on peer collaboration in Chapter 7):

> Students need experiences that will engage them meaningfully; this will happen best with an activity that is tied to specific learning goals and content that is important for students to learn.

- **Make models.** Build them, draw them, or create them digitally. There are so many possibilities: models of math reasoning when solving proportion problems, structure of a school, state, or national government authority, making a decision about a classroom protocol, negotiating a compromise, or surviving middle school.
- **Embark on field trips.** Visit and learn outside of class. Instead of only learning about plants from print material or videos, grow a garden, or take a day to explore plants in an outdoor area near your school. To begin your study about animal behaviors, visit

the zoo to observe the behaviors in action. Visit places that have resources, features, people, or operations that relate to what you want students to learn: galleries, museums, heritage sites, businesses, government offices, farms, dams, bridges, waterfalls, parks, and factories.

- **Include experiments of all sorts.** Have students **do** the work. Dissect worms, flowers, or squid. Apply the scientific method for experiments to other subject areas. Lots of critical thinking and planning will go into setting a hypothesis, identifying variables, holding certain variables static, and so on.

- **Incorporate role-play.** Move students beyond simply reading about or discussing a situation, event, concept, or job; get them living it. While role-play is often associated with historical events, it can apply to many other areas, including weather reports, safety procedures, conflict resolution, mock science experiments, and town council debates or press conferences. Students might role-play a school board discussing a proposed rule change or use math, science, and language-arts skills to play detectives solving a mystery. A quick caution: Role-playing historical figures can be sensitive, as interpretations vary and it can unintentionally reinforce misconceptions or stereotypes.

- **Integrate art.** Use the arts (drama, mime, dance, music, painting, drawing, sculpture) to depict or explain academic concepts. After reading a novel, ask students to use paint, sculpture, or a graphic design program to present a visual interpretation of a character or to represent the plot line of the story. Be careful to make sure you are still measuring student mastery toward the standard and not spending too much time on activities that do not help students learn the standard. When I (Laurie) taught 12th-grade English, I had students make three-dimensional models of one of the characters from *The Canterbury Tales*. It was a favorite project every year, and I ended up with quite the collection of very well-crafted Wife of Baths, Knights, Millers, and Friars. Looking back, I think about how much time students spent on these characters and wonder how much of that supported actually learning English language arts content.

- **Explore businesses.** Students can plan (or mock create) a simple mini-business or evaluate an existing business in your area. They can create a mock bank, hiring staff, setting up banking operations and processes, accounts, and ways to carry out transactions. Students can deposit income, design budgets, plan savings, and spend "money."

- **Expand community and global understanding.** Identify, investigate, and analyze situations, problems, and challenges that connect students to their community or the wider world. Have students explore how these situations affect them and what they can do to contribute to solutions. (Look for local opportunities through civic organizations, food banks, or literacy programs).

- **Learn from interviews.** Students identify and interview people who can contribute to what they are learning. The *Foxfire* series is an amazing example of how this type of learning can make a difference. In 1966, an English teacher and his students in Northeast Georgia founded a quarterly magazine as a vehicle to learn the required English curriculum but also to teach others about their Appalachian culture. It became a national best seller and funded the Foxfire Museum and Heritage Center that still exists today.[6] Look for ways to connect interviews to content and standards students are learning. In U.S. history class, students might find relatives, neighbors, or residents in senior citizen homes who will talk about their experiences in a war or other key events in the country's history. When learning about important medical discoveries in science class, students might interview medical professionals who can tell how these technologies, medications, or procedures affect their work today. Match other interviews to content learning areas through experts in any field.

- **Learn through service.** Set up effective service-learning projects that connect academic learning with real community needs, allowing students to apply classroom learning in meaningful, practical ways. A political science class might register elderly voters while gathering insights on policy issues important to them. Health science students might organize rural health fairs to provide screenings and wellness education. Elementary math students could organize a charity bake sale or book drive, using math to budget, count donations, and track totals.

- **Incorporate gamification.** Capitalize on students' interest in video games. Use elements of video games (challenges, levels, points, rewards, and collaboration) to make learning engaging and interactive. A science teacher could design a "mission" where students work in teams to solve environmental mysteries, earning digital badges for discovering key concepts.

Keep Students Engaged from Start to Finish

Great teaching and learning does not begin and end with a dynamic start to a captivating lesson. Engagement is sustained through any lesson, project, or unit when the entire experience (from planning, introducing, carrying out, and wrapping up) is accompanied by the teacher's clear presentation and ongoing energy. Plan and structure each learning experience to offer inspiration, guidelines, support, formative assessment for each step of the process, and opportunities to share outcomes and products. To keep the learning active and keep students engaged from the first to the final moment of a lesson:

- Actively involve students in preparations and plans for learning experiences:

- Identify and discuss clear, transparent expectations, goals, and purposes of the activity.

- Design and discuss requirements and boundaries for the learning process (time, restraint, spaces, organizational procedures, record-keeping, behaviors, strategies needed).

- Check to see that students understand the choices and freedoms (and boundaries) they have in meeting expectations of the assignment.

- Brainstorm (with students) questions, suggestions, options, and ideas to get students started. Provide helpful and relevant resources and guidance. Allow as much flexibility as possible for students to investigate areas they choose (again, within the boundaries of the learning experience).

- Describe and show students how their learning will be assessed (when, how, and by what specific criteria).

- Build in and explain to students processes for monitoring progress, giving and receiving feedback, and making changes or additions to the learning plan.

- Build capacity for the learning to come. Define difficult vocabulary in advance. Provide students with a guide and process for approaching problems or a written selection of problem-solving strategies with a graphic organizer for student thinking or a rubric for a category of tasks (writing an essay, presenting an argument, conducting an inquiry). Identify meaningful analogies that can bring clarity for students (*Think of the human circulatory system as a map of roadways*). Sequence a lesson with the concept of: I do, we do, you all do, you do.

- Continue their active involvement with in-process monitoring. Check in frequently on their progress to assess student learning. Ask such questions as *Where are you in your plan? Do you feel satisfied with your progress? What have you learned or accomplished so far? Is anything confusing or challenging you? What help do you need? What will you do next?* Use some tools you prepared ahead of time for your monitoring or student self-monitoring (rubrics, checklists, steps to a goal, or list of questions for students to follow).

* Wrap up the learning experience with practices that continue active thinking and practices from students–self-reflection, discussion, demonstration, and other forms of sharing. (See Chapter 14 for more about student reflection.) These will allow students to process, more deeply understand, evaluate, and apply their learning. Check on their ability to express what they learned and why it matters:

  * Can students verbalize or demonstrate what they learned and how?

  * Can students describe the value and usefulness of what they are learning? Ask them to write or discuss (large group, small group, or with a peer) some questions: *What happened? What did you expect (and why)? What was unexpected (and why)? What was most important? What do you now assume or want to tell others since taking part in this experience? What difference does this make? Why does it matter? If you had to do this again, what would you do differently? What advice would you give future students who engage with this? How does this connect to real life? How does this connect to something else you know? What else do you wonder? What would you like to do, try, or learn next about this?*

One year when Laurie was a middle school principal, 8th grad-ers were about to study electricity. Before starting the unit, their teachers built excitement for the topic by taking them to see a live performance by Arc Attack (where performers illustrate physics concepts through live demonstration—like a Tesla Coil Show). Seeing electricity in a dynamic, tangible way, beyond simply flipping a light switch, created a powerful connection that brought the whole topic of electricity alive in a new way. The vivid images of electricity at work triggered excitement and sparked their imaginations. Students returned to class full of wonder and ideas. Teachers grabbed hold of their enthusiasm by gathering their comments and questions. These questions triggered research, projects, and experiments to find out more about what cool and useful things electricity can do and how.

ENGAGE Students with Exploration

My (Patti's) 6th graders were studying electricity through hands-on activities—exploring conductors, insulators, circuits, energy sources, and more. The materials were kept in bins, easy to grab when it was time for science.

One day after returning from lunch, I found a playground aide scolding three usually well-behaved boys outside the classroom. She had discovered them inside unsupervised during recess and was quite upset, demanding I "do something!" I brought the boys inside and asked what they were doing. Excitedly, they said, "Look what we made!" During lunch, they'd come up with an idea, slipped back into the room, gathered supplies, and built a working doorbell for the classroom, complete with wiring, a switch, and hidden batteries.

The aide clearly expected me to give them consequences, but how could I? They had applied what they were learning in a creative, real-world way, the kind of learning we all hope for. I simply reminded them not to come in without permission and explained that, if they'd asked, I'd have gladly stayed to supervise.

All these years later, I'm still in touch with two of those boys. Now successful men in their fifties, they've continued to explore, create, and grow. Evidentially, that curiosity they showed in 6th grade never dimmed.

Exploration is an active learning approach that engages students and expands and deepens required concepts and content in classroom lessons. Fueled by students' curiosity and innate drive to make sense of their world, exploration often takes the form of self-directed or collaborative inquiries and projects that spur creativity and innovation. It draws students to investigate something of personal interest related to what they're learning in a class, delve into real-world experiences, and learn about diverse perspectives and cultures.[1]

The attitudes, skills, and abilities students develop when they learn within a culture of exploration are foundational to lives and futures. As educators, we should always help students develop these in a world that is rapidly changing. When we think back on the worlds we grew up in (Patti, mostly in the 60s; Laurie, mostly in the 80s), we are awed by the magnitude of the changes that have occurred. If we hadn't developed the desire to continually grow and learn, we wouldn't have become as successful in our careers or personal lives as we are today. Helping our students cultivate mindsets and skills of exploration gives them a strong foundation for lifelong learning.

> Helping our students cultivate mindsets and skills of exploration gives them a strong foundation for lifelong learning.

Put It Into Practice

Set the stage and tone for exploration

Learning through exploration flourishes in an environment where students feel safe, their curiosity is encouraged, their questions are valued, their autonomy is promoted, and they feel supported to take cognitive risks.[2] These actions promote such an environment:

- Be a role model for exploration and innovation.
  - Be enthusiastic in three areas: your content and teaching, learning in general, and learning and sharing with your students. Allow students to see how much you enjoy teaching and learning more about how to do it well. Show students that learning can be fun, meaningful, and rewarding. It's difficult to disengage when you're enthusiastic about something.
  - Let students know about (appropriate) failures you have experienced and challenges you have overcome. Share anecdotes of other people with similar experiences making mistakes and learning from them. Let students tell their own (appropriate) stories of overcoming challenges.
  - Participate in professional development to enhance exploratory learning; investigate processes and ideas for discovery learning; stay up to date on new trends, techniques, and technologies in your field.
- Build attitudes, skills, processes, and questions students need for exploration.
  - **Attitudes:** Cultivate a culture in which students wonder and hypothesize, where they are eager to find answers to their questions about their school learning content and the world. Fill your classroom with questions that inspire wondering and hypothesizing. *What do you know about ____? What do you not know? How would you go about ____? What do you think might happen if?* Let students know that it is safe to think outside the box, come up with unusual ideas, or try something that doesn't work.
  - **Skills:** Plan lessons that require curiosity, investigation,

experimenting, and risk-taking. Instead of teaching students a method or formula for finding the area of a triangle in 4th grade, begin with an exploration. Students already understand the concept of area and the formula for area of a rectangle. Give them large paper triangles, and pair students to discover what a formula might be for finding its area. Students draw and measure, trying different possibilities, many of them not giving an answer. A 6th-grade teacher teaching a lesson on the cause of rainbows starts class not with a textbook or video but with students' previous knowledge about light being a combination of colors that can be separated. That is followed by a series of explorations with glasses of water, magnifying glasses, prisms, lights, and sunshine through the window, capped off with an outdoor trip to turn on a sprinkler placed where sun can shine through it.

- **Processes:** Teach about identifying a purpose, setting goals, making a plan, finding the right resources, being open to new things showing up they did not expect, dealing with obstacles and setbacks, reflecting on work, and sharing what they learned. Help them see how their exploration questions can grow out of a topic the class has studied. Use an example to work together through the processes of exploring. At each phase, including setbacks, discuss ways to proceed.

- **Questions:** Get students brainstorming about kinds of questions to ask that could become the basis of explorations. For practice, give a topic they have studied or are about to study and have students offer questions. Change to another topic and then another. Add your suggestions to theirs. This will push them into investigating, researching, imagining, following clues, and discovering.

- Collaborate with students to set exploration guidelines and boundaries. Refine these until they are clear and easy for students to state and follow. Set processes for exploring alone and processes for students exploring together in pairs or small groups or for collaborating (digitally) with persons outside of school.

Build Excitement About Questions that Inspire Exploration

A question is often the starting point for most explorations. Classroom learning sparks curiosity, exciting students and prompting them to wonder. From this initial question, students develop a learning goal and begin planning their investigation. Of course there are hundreds of questions that can be generated from any lesson: *What is quicksand, and could I drown in it? Why is physical education necessary for children? Why do people have fingerprints, and why does it matter? Why are human populations more dense along rivers? How can I disprove that argument we just read?*

Provide Guided Instruction for Exploration Processes

An exploration grows out of good instruction; it follows from a basic assignment or mastery of a new concept or skill, and it can be integrated into or flow from any lesson. Exploration is inspired by the satisfaction of engagement with a topic combined with the acquisition of some new understandings and skills. With newly-gained confidence and ideas, students are eager to learn more and ready to follow their curiosity to create, discover, innovate, or put new skills to work on something bigger. To guide students' exploration:

+ For any unit of study, be ready with some exploration ideas. Ask questions or problems to kick off an exploration, but allow students to build explorations around their own questions or prompts, too. Share a variety of resources on connected topics (posters, artifacts, food samples, guest speakers, games, short videos, photographs—anything that might spark a question or interest).

- Guide students in choosing what to explore by noticing what captures their interest during or after learning activities. Ask them what they'd like to learn or do next or how they might apply their learning. Encourage choice and passion in their explorations while also providing direction to ensure their work deepens, broadens, and adds value to what they've learned in the classroom.

In the middle school where Patti was principal, students in an integrated language arts/social studies class studying early civilizations were learning about ancient Egypt and the effect that civilization had on the world. After studying broad information about the culture, students launched into deeper investigation, exploring questions of their individual interests: *How and why were the pyramids built? Why and where did the ancient Egyptians build ships and become explorers? How did the explorations of the ancient Egyptians affect other civilizations in the region? What was the meaning of the mummification concept and how did the process work? Why and how was the Aswan dam built? Why were temples taken down during the building of the dam?*

- Ensure student exploration is worth the time and effort. Begin with simple projects, and increase complexity as students gain experience. Remind students to explore topics that expand what they learned already and are meaningful and cognitively challenging. (They can ask themselves: *Will the question I pursue lead to finding out how and why something matters? Will I have to push my brain beyond what I already know about something to learn more about it or understand it in a new way? Will I have to apply some knowledge that I have to a new situation? Will I need to analyze data or information, draw conclusions, or evaluate the worth of information?)*

- Give students time to plan their explorations. A good plan saves time, reduces confusion, and keeps them engaged. Co-design a digital or paper format where they identify learning goals, needed materials, steps, required skills, sources of information, steps to take, and places and ways to monitor and reflect on each step. Provide clear, project-specific requirements such as needed references, format expectations, presentation options, or length. Teach students to clearly state the purpose and specific curriculum-connected goals for the tasks.

- Work with students to establish systems for monitoring, reflecting on, and evaluating their work. Before they begin, ensure they know how to monitor and reflect on their progress using tools such as step-by-step templates with reflection spaces, task checklists, or a student-friendly rubric tailored to the assignment.

- Allow for changes, challenges, and growth during exploration. The process can be messy as plans shift, setbacks occur, new possibilities emerge, and products turn out differently than expected. Perhaps two students researching arguments for allowing cell phones at school shifted their focus after seeing how people felt about the issue. So instead, they explored and surveyed that topic.

- Share, discuss, and reflect on the process. The entire exploration process is highly engaging for students; yet this final step boosts it even higher. Together, reflecting and telling others about the experience completes the cycle of metacognition that is deeply embedded in exploration. (See Chapter 13 for more about metacognition.)

- Create a system for students to share their explorations. Teaching others is a key part of the Inquiry Method. Authentic audiences are powerful. Students should state their original question, present their answer, explain their thinking and its real-world relevance, and share their surprises and challenges. Whether through demonstrations, videos, visual walk-throughs, speeches, or simulations, sharing their work deepens learning and boosts motivation.

Welcome and Suggest Multiple Ways to Explore

There are unlimited places, spaces, and ideas to explore, and as many ways to do so. Here are some approaches:

* Explore and learn outside the classroom with field trips or visits to a museum, local historical sites, musical or theater performances, a park, or a business. Let students brainstorm a list of interesting places to explore.
* Give students chances to examine a variety of career paths that have connection to things they have studied. They can determine what skills and knowledge would be needed to pursue a career of their interest.
* Let students know about the many possibilities for taking part in national or international student competitions, many of which are online (Kangaroo Math Competition, Write the World International Writing Contest, the Google Science Fair, etc.). You'll find dozens more possibilities with an online search.
* Suggest sites for taking virtual tours that explore a topic they studied (through Earth's atmosphere, a human bloodstream, a deep-sea diver's investigation of a shipwreck, or following the life of an elephant for a week). Again, you'll find dozens of such tours and virtual field trips with an online search.
* Encourage exploration through varied media that leads to real innovation:

- Sculptures (straws, wire, marshmallows, clay, toothpicks, or digital manipulations) to demonstrate science concepts or geometric problems
- 3-D models (digital or physical) of geographical or math features
- Online surveys to connect to learning about statistics
- Musical or artistic compositions that teach or expand a concept
- Webpages that expand on a lesson
- Reflections, quizzes, or other assessments fitted to a topic
- An educational video or video game
- A scavenger hunt to find objects relevant to the topic
- A chatbot, video, or tutorial to teach someone about the topic

When I (Laurie) was a 12th-grade English teacher, school started in early August each year. On the minds of most seniors I taught was the looming college applications process. The majority of students in my class had aspirations of going to a post-secondary school yet struggled with where to start. In my first-year teaching seniors, I realized that so many of them had no idea how to navigate the application process. I decided then that a primary focus for the opening months of our 12th-grade English class was going to be the college application process.

With English language arts concepts and goals in mind, I developed a checklist and rubric of the full process for students. (As a young teacher in graduate school, I wasn't that far removed from the process myself.) We took time each week, along with our regular curriculum goals, to talk about, plan, and work on the many components of the college application process. Even for students who may not have been interested in going to college immediately after school or ever, they were still learning about English language arts content as well as opportunities that existed should they choose that route later in life.

From making a list of colleges of interest, writing personal essays, requesting letters of recommendations, writing a resume (including lists of extracurricular involvement, honors and awards, work history, and community and volunteer work) to actually completing the application and submitting transcripts and standardized test scores, students did it all. The final project was always due by September 30 and required a fully-completed application, three personal essays that had been submitted for grading, feedback, and revisions (I gave them a list of common questions, or they could use ones from actual applications they were completing), a full resume, and three letters of recommendation. Whether students actually submitted the completed application was their decision.

While initially students complained about having to do all this work ("I only need one essay for my application." "My application doesn't require a resume." "I don't know where I want to apply."), every year, students thanked me for requiring this process. I think parents were even more appreciative of the guidance, feedback, and accountability it placed on their children as they explored post-secondary options. Almost all the students actually ended up submitting full applications by the early decision deadline and/or used the polished essays, resumes, and letters of recommendation for numerous other opportunities such as honors, scholarships, and job applications.

Students in future classes (and their parents) began asking me about the project before school even started each year. What I realized is that almost all students had a strong desire to explore opportunities for after high school, but most really needed strong guidance, support, and time to get them started. Encouraging students to engage in and explore takes intentional planning and effort, but the rewards when they begin to see their efforts pay off far outlast the work involved (for both teacher and students).

PART 3

Empower!

Introduction

WHAT?
A Picture of Empowerment

Empowerment goes beyond even the highest levels of engagement and begins when students initiate and follow their own ideas and interests, taking ownership of their learning. Effective schools and teachers recognize that when students have meaningful control over parts of their educational processes, they become deeply invested, and their potential for growth expands dramatically.

Student empowerment is, at its core, a central goal of education. Yet it is often misunderstood or underdeveloped. While the idea of empowering students may feel unsettling to some educators (because they possibly fear that this may diminish their own authority or because they may be uncertain as to how to handle this process), a clear understanding of what it means and how it works reveals that it rightly deserves to be seen as one of education's most important aims.

Definitions

Student empowerment: setting beliefs and processes by which students gain more agency over their learning and school life, with educators helping them build confidence and abilities to control their lives and contribute to decisions about their learning

Student disempowerment: a state in which students feel stripped of power, autonomy, influence, or control in their life or environment

More about the Meaning of Student Empowerment

Empowerment is often misunderstood. Some definitions of empowerment suggest that power or authority is **granted** from one person to another. In reality, students already possess the right and the innate capacity to have control over their lives (within the limits of being minors, of developmental capabilities, and with guiding adults) and to influence their surroundings. Every effective teacher knows there is power within students. Sometimes it's visible and vibrant, but at other times, it's hidden, subtle, passive, or expressed in unproductive ways.

When we "empower students," we create the conditions and supports that enable them to build confidence, develop skills, increase agency (capacity to take ownership and active participation in shaping their learning journeys), and use their personal power in appropriate and productive ways. In doing so, teachers **share** authority, responsibility, and decision-making, providing students with authentic opportunities to exercise that power in ways that are developmentally appropriate and do not diminish the teacher's role.

> Every effective teacher knows there is power within students. Sometimes it's visible and vibrant, but at other times, it's hidden, subtle, passive, or expressed in unproductive ways.

Empowering students is about the teacher stepping back some of the time. Teachers remove tight controls and obstacles that thwart students' authority over their learning and school lives. This approach makes the empowering process possible; it welcomes students' active roles in making choices and achieving competency and expands their stake in the meaningful workings of their personal learning and classroom life. The teacher is still present to guide and instruct in the skills students need to use their power. There will be multiple situations in which teachers have clear authority: enforcing school rules and proper conduct (discipline), deciding what's being taught that week, assessment and grading, and other administrative and curricular elements.

Envision students as prime movers within clear guidelines. Student empowerment involves letting students set the tone as much as possible for what they need, what they want to explore, and how they want to learn, evaluate, and share what they learn. As details in the following chapters will show, this is a gradual process of giving students training and practice in taking on more and more responsibility and having greater and greater agency as they mature and build behaviors for empowerment.

Student empowerment does NOT mean taking away the power of teachers, diminishing respect for teachers, or diminishing the value of teachers' professional preparation and teaching skills. Teachers do not need to be wary of student empowerment.

WHY?
The Power of Student Empowerment

Student empowerment is the pathway to true ownership of learning and forms the foundation for autonomy and essential life skills. By inspiring and guiding students to explore, expand, and apply that power in healthy and responsible ways, we help them grow into independent adults capable of making decisions, directing their own lives, and contributing meaningfully to an ever-changing world.

Some Discoveries about Empowerment

Countless research studies affirm the positive value of student empowerment. Here are some general findings that reveal the impact:[1]

1. Students' sense of the amount of power and control they have in classroom life and learning significantly affects the quality and depth of their learning and level of achievement as well as their engagement and behavior in classrooms.

2. Teachers' beliefs about student empowerment influence their teaching decisions and behaviors.

3. The success of student empowerment correlates directly to the level of teacher support for students to increase and use their power. As a result, students may feel more empowered in some classes than others, depending on the teacher and the classroom's power dynamics (how power is shared, negotiated, and expressed among the teacher, individual students, and student groups—the sense of who has control in different situations and how that power is used). These dynamics are often felt or perceived more than they are visibly seen.

4. Many teachers fear that student empowerment will take away teacher control. Empowering students does not disempower teachers. According to researcher Catherine Broom, "Sharing power does not mean a person has less. Instead, teachers maintain and gain power by sharing power, for power is more than a top-down form of control."[2] She explains that power is a multifaceted ability to influence one's environment, a spider web of variables that influence each other.

5. Many traditional teaching practices have the opposite effect of student empowerment by leaving all decisions about learning processes and classroom protocols in the hands of the teacher.

6. Student empowerment does not diminish academic rigor. In fact, as students gain more ownership of their learning and increase belief in their capabilities, they are more invested in working hard to meet challenges and to find the purpose and meaning in their learning.

7. Student empowerment is an ongoing process. It can be developed in increments, with more opportunities for it offered as skills grow. A student's sense of empowerment or disempowerment is not static: It can fluctuate, depending on a host of different settings and circumstances.

Benefits of Empowerment

When positively empowered, students are more likely to:[3]

+ See a sense of purpose in what they are learning and understand how it matters in their lives and others' lives.
+ Set personal goals and self-expectations beyond what is set for them by teachers.
+ Actively and productively engage with others and with causes, projects, organizations, and situations in their wider environment; collaborate, work, plan, negotiate, and reach consensus with others.
+ Examine and revise perceptions of others; get to know and understand peers better.
+ Speak up; use their voices confidently to express their insights, questions, and experiences; voice affirmation for and learn about others; and learn what they want to know more about.
+ Develop and effectively use leadership skills.
+ Use their personal power in positive ways that improve themselves and make a positive difference beyond themselves.
+ Experience and display:

- Sense of belonging; greater satisfaction, optimism, and enjoyment in school.
- Self-management and proactive, positive behavior.
- Autonomy, self-confidence, self-belief, and self-esteem.
- Academic interest and growth.
- Intrinsic motivation and eagerness to take risks, explore, research, and discover.
- Understanding and appreciation of their own insights and capabilities.
- Belief that they can make a difference.

Consequences of Disempowerment

Life for students in and out of school is complex and filled with challenges. Social issues, troubling societal events, personal worries, and academic pressures cause many students to feel overwhelmed and powerless. Some of the circumstances are out of the control of educators who care for students. We can, however, pay attention to signs of disempowerment and employ effective strategies shown to boost students' personal power and teach them how to use it. Furthermore, we can be alert to factors within the learning environment, content, and experiences that may contribute to disempowerment. Here are some indications and results of disempowerment:[4]

- Withdrawal; feelings of exclusion or marginalization
- Loss of confidence and self-belief
- Sense of weakness, insignificance, or inadequacy
- Belief that ideas and participation are not valued
- Fear, frustration, or disappointment
- Feeling overwhelmed, hopeless, or helpless
- Anger, outbursts, or inappropriate uses of power

It is also important to note that the benefits of empowerment are missing from students who perceive themselves to be powerless. The good news is that any experiences of empowerment can begin to reverse the characteristics above and begin to yield the benefits of empowerment.

HOW?
The Pathway to Student Empowerment

What role do we, as educators, play in helping students discover their individual power, understand how it can influence their learning, their lives, and the lives of others, and develop and use it in positive ways?

Begin with a genuine belief that students' power should be strengthened within the school and classroom. Recognize that within a culture where adults share authority, students can be equipped to take an active role in shaping their own learning and lives and to make positive contributions to their communities. Create a safe, inclusive environment where students can exercise their power appropriately and confidently, trusting that everyone's influence will be guided and used for good.

In Part 3 of the book, we explore these elements of student empowerment and more through **transferring more authority and responsibility, meaningful learning, challenge and success, self-reflection and self-evaluation,** and **technology.** Each of the following chapters (11-15) describes a specific, concrete action with supporting strategies to increase and sustain positive student empowerment. The recommended behaviors and practices are observable to our students, ourselves, and others. They can be intentionally practiced, honed, and, in many cases, measured.

Although Part 3 focuses on empowerment, you'll find that the mindset and practices here also trigger student **engagement** and boost the processes of reaching high **expectations.**

EMPOWER Students with Authority and Responsibility

One year, I (Patti) was invited by the local humane society to partner with them on a new program that paired at-risk students with shelter dogs needing basic manners training. The goal was simple: teaching commands like "sit," "stay," and "come" would help the dogs get adopted. Since our alternative education program sat just across the street and had room for activity, we gladly joined in.

With parent permission, students were each paired with a dog and, twice a week for six weeks, worked with a professional trainer to teach and practice skills. The program ended with a "dog show" for families and staff, where the dogs proudly demonstrated what they'd learned.

Students beamed with pride, not just for their dogs but for themselves. They'd taken responsibility, built confidence, and seen their efforts pay off. By the end, every dog was adopted (some by the very students who trained them).

Empowering students with authority and responsibility allows students to take ownership of their learning and assume more meaningful roles and control in their academic life and in their classroom, school, and community. The idea of student empowerment is often misunderstood. It doesn't mean simply giving students power; it means helping them build and appropriately use it. This means teachers must shift from making every decision to guiding students in making thoughtful choices that give them more control in many areas of their classroom life and learning.

Jonathan Erwin, author of *The Classroom of Choice*, writes about students' need for power and about different ways power is used and shared. His work is based on William Glasser's identification of "the need for power through cooperation and competency" as one of the five basic human needs: survival (physical wellbeing and safety); love and belonging; power and self-worth; freedom; and fun and enjoyment.[1] Erwin describes three kinds of power:[2]

- **Power over:** the urge to control others because one believes it's good for the other person or perhaps for personal satisfaction. *The teacher makes all the rules for learning and behavior in the classroom, explains them, and expects students to follow them.*
- **Power with:** power achieved in cooperation with others. *The teacher and students join in a discussion about what academic and behavioral protocols are needed in the classroom, agree on them, decide how they will be practiced and monitored, and set a process for all parties to share feedback over time about how the protocols are working. The teacher may contribute a few non-negotiable protocols but only when accompanied by explanations and reasons.*
- **Power within:** power that a person feels or gains from competence or accomplishments. *As a student works hard to accomplish goals and succeeds at managing more learning independently, she*

becomes more aware of and empowered by her growth and capabilities in academic and behavioral skills.

Erwin's book encourages teachers to provide multiple opportunities daily for students to observe in the teacher and to gain for themselves the second two kinds of power. He explains that, when the teacher backs off from *power over* and models *power within* and *power with* (shared power), students learn to meet their needs for power through choosing the second two kinds of power rather than trying to exert control over others.[3]

Put It Into Practice

Examine Your Personal Understanding of Empowerment

When students feel capable and trusted with real responsibility, their confidence grows. That sense of agency (capacity to act or have power–particularly in regard to ownership of their learning) leads to genuine enthusiasm, authentic engagement, and deeper learning. Like any important skill, empowerment must be taught through intentional instruction, solid practices, and the right support to help students build and apply it effectively. But before teaching these skills, teachers must examine their own beliefs about what it means to empower students and then determine practices they are already doing as well as what they might stop or do differently. Consider:

> Like any important skill, empowerment must be taught through intentional instruction, solid practices, and the right support to help students build and apply it effectively.

+ When we empower students, we build their confidence and capability by gradually sharing responsibilities that teachers once managed alone. Do your classroom procedures, practices, and instruction promote more *power over* students, *power within* each student, or *power with* one another?

+ Limiting *power over* students and balancing building *power within* and *power with* develops true empowerment. Do you work for such a balance in the ways you manage and teach?

+ Both teachers and students become partners in learning, each contributing to success and independence. Do you conceive of student empowerment this way?

+ And it's not just about teachers sharing power with students. Students also learn to share authority and responsibility with one another, which makes the classroom community even stronger. Does this describe the culture of your classroom?

Expand Student Empowerment

Success at empowering students is rooted in the values, norms, attitudes, and processes of the classroom and school. Here are some ways to lay a foundation for empowerment and build upon it:

+ Set the environment for appropriate and increasing empowerment. Some important underlying conditions are:

  + Students have a competent teacher, knowledgeable and committed, who provides a wide range of options and opportunities for increasing student empowerment and who skillfully teaches, guides, and supports the process of increasing empowerment.

  + Students feel known, valued, and supported as individuals beyond their achievements or behavior. In collaboration, teachers and students set practices for acknowledging such things as each other's passions, interests, curiosity, sense of humor, patience, unique insights, or creativity.

- The classroom fosters strong teacher-student and peer relationships, connection, and community. Teachers and students together brainstorm (and put to use) ways to increase belonging, trust, and a sense of "us."
- The learning environment builds positive identity and agency, helping students develop self-regulation, self-advocacy, and confidence.
- Classroom management centers on a community of engagement and empowerment, reducing the need for strict rules and consequences. In classroom discussions, the teacher and students regularly reflect on how life is going in the classroom, listening to each other and solving issues together.
- Intentional teacher planning identifies when students can take ownership (when the teacher can step back, supported by clear, practiced boundaries for increasing student power). This involves thinking through assignments or practices to identify what the signs will be that students are ready for more (or complete) autonomy in a given situation.
- Student voice and choice are embedded throughout learning, with authentic purposes and real impact.
- The teacher models healthy, respectful use of power and addresses misuse when it occurs.

- Gradually share responsibility and authority with students. Shift from compliance to empowerment by giving students increasing choice and control as their confidence and skills grow. Stay present to guide and support, but resist stepping in too quickly. Let them work through challenges and setbacks. Provide tools for planning, problem-solving, and reflection so they can manage frustration and learn from mistakes. True empowerment means helping students handle all parts of authority, even the hard parts! Here's an example of that shift:

- For the process of accomplishing a particular goal in a classroom, the teacher usually provides the goal, purpose, step-by-step template, materials, guided reflection questions, and assessment. Students are familiar with this structure and understand goal-setting and planning.
- For the next task, however, the teacher begins to shift responsibility to students by giving them a blank template to create their own steps after the task is explained. Instead of rescuing hesitant students, the teacher pairs them with peers and guides them to review and refine their sequence.
- Once students understand the planning process, the teacher gradually adds new responsibilities, one at a time, such as choosing and stating a goal for a specific broader assignment, explaining its importance, and selecting some (eventually all) of the materials.
- Over the next days or weeks, students gain more autonomy: developing reflection questions for use during and after the task, self-reflecting, contributing ideas for assessments, helping choose (from a negotiated list) how the task will be assessed, and self-evaluating their own work and progress.
- Eventually, many students can self-manage the entire process of setting goals, planning, completing tasks, and evaluating their work. The teacher still monitors, checks in, and assists as needed, after giving students time and strategies to work through challenges independently or with peers.

Let Students Do What They CAN do

Don't do anything for them that they can do for themselves is often said about toddlers and pre-schoolers. But it's even more true as students proceed through school. There is so much that we adults continue to do for students that they are capable of doing themselves—especially with appropriate teaching and monitoring. Whenever possible, look for areas where the teacher does not need to have the *power over* something and can transfer most or all responsibility for a task to students:

- Identify, strengthen, and expand student empowerment:
    - Start by identifying what authority and responsibilities already belong to students in your classroom; take stock of how empowered they are right now. (Look for student autonomy in keeping track of assignments, choosing from a range of ways to complete a task, finding resources for a task, setting a goal for a task and following a plan to meet it, or bringing correct supplies to class without being reminded). Create a list, and involve your students in the process.
    - Next, work with students to identify tasks or decisions they could take on that the teacher usually handles. Look for places where you can safely loosen control without compromising student or teacher confidentiality. Simply involving students in this reflection is empowering and often eye-opening and freeing for teachers. When students suggest or volunteer for new responsibilities, they're usually more motivated to show they can handle them. In a classroom where the teacher normally leads daily discussions, students might take turns facilitating the conversation, tracking key ideas, or choosing which texts to analyze next. Over time, this shared leadership strengthens both competence and community.
    - Finally, build on or create practices that strengthen students' *power within themselves*—the confidence and capability gained through responsibility and success. By definition, this kind of power grows through success. Make a habit of recognizing it. Once a week, students can briefly acknowledge

a capability they noticed in a classmate. At the end of each day or class or week, students can write or share a quick note about a success or new skill (not just completing a task but achieving something that stretches their learning). *I struggled with two-variable equations at first, so I reviewed the steps, broke each equation down, compared my work to samples, and asked a peer to give feedback. I checked each solution by working the problem backward and looked for mistakes when the solution didn't work in reverse. By the end of class, I had solved several correctly.*

Here's a bonus: when these practices are shared and collaborative, they also develop *power with* others, and the result is collective empowerment.

- Work with your students to outline the requirements of some tasks:
    - Basic classroom tasks: Students are capable of responsibly handling most "housekeeping" tasks in the classroom.
    - Decision-making and planning for classroom operations: Students can and should take part in designing routines, procedures, and norms that guide classroom life, including how they work with and treat one another and the teacher. When students help shape these systems, they feel invested in following and maintaining them.
    - Operational and organizational procedures for their personal learning: Given a selection of tasks that can lead to meeting a learning goal and given meaningful options and possibilities for resources and processes, students can sometimes or often:
        - Set goals and plan learning. Choose topics that fit the content, identify specific learning targets, and create a plan to reach them.

- Select resources and strategies. Decide which materials, tools, activities, and processes to use for researching, learning, and completing tasks.
- Monitor their progress. Use guides or checklists to track growth, seek help when needed, and make adjustments along the way.
- Demonstrate and reflect. Decide how to show learning, reflect on progress using a guide, and evaluate results.
- Share their learning progression. Teach what they've learned to others and take the lead in conferences with teachers and families.

- Operational and organizational procedures for learning together (pairs, groups) without the teacher's help: Given a joint learning goal and teacher guidelines, students can increase their *power with* (achieved in cooperation with others) as well as *power within* when they:
  - Use peer tutors (in their grade level or at other levels).
  - Plan and conduct collaborative learning activities.
  - Plan and conduct class or team meetings or celebrations.
  - Engage in debate and lively discussions in which they share opinions, justify perspectives, and ask meaningful questions of one another.
  - Reflect on and evaluate any of the above learning experiences.

We acknowledge that turning over more responsibility to students for tasks may increase the time it takes to complete them. As teachers, we are more efficient at designing routines and better at thinking ahead to avoid confusion; students don't possess this same capacity. But if we see the value in students learning these processes and growing in autonomy and agency, we know that the extended time is worth it.

Spending the time leads to what we say we want: for our students to become more engaged, confident, and empowered.

Join Forces with Students

Build shared authority and responsibility to increase their *power with* (power shared in cooperation with others). This is *interdependence.* It is at the core of shared authority. And there are many wonderful opportunities for teachers and students to be empowered together:

- Discuss with students the idea of shared power. Use the same process suggested in the previous section (where you expand the number of tasks for which students can take full responsibility—*power over*). Begin here by identifying practices in your classroom life and learning that already share responsibility between teacher and students. Then discuss areas where shared power can expand. Invite students to contribute their observations and experiences of this (designing some lessons, teaching key vocabulary or concepts, giving feedback on student outcomes, creating rubrics, and planning and conducting class or team meetings).
- Use your collaborative ideas to expand students' *power with* others. Students can co-create or co-demonstrate with teachers:
  - **Modeling and accountability:** Teachers and students model expectations for one another and take shared responsibility for upholding class norms through consistent actions and peer accountability structures. A teacher can model respect by addressing a behavior issue privately to protect the student's dignity and avoid embarrassment. A student can model accountability in a group project by making sure everyone's voice is included in planning, ensuring all members participate in reflecting on the work or final product

and reminding the group of protocols for interdependence in group work.

- **Leadership and collaboration:** Students develop leadership skills through participation in class meetings, peer groups, and collaborative learning experiences that promote teamwork and shared decision-making.
- **Problem-solving and self-regulation:** The teacher and students together practice conflict resolution and coping and demonstrate self-management strategies to maintain a positive, productive environment.
- **Goal-setting and feedback:** Students use clear frameworks for setting goals, tracking progress, reflecting on learning, and giving and receiving feedback.
- **Learning design, presentation, and assessment:** Students engage in lesson planning, create rubrics, and use self-monitoring and reflection tools to evaluate their learning and share knowledge with peers.
- **Balance and community:** Classroom plans intentionally include brain breaks and social interactions to support well-being and connection.

Strengthen Students' Internal Power

The third kind of power that Jonathan Erwin described is power *within*—the inner sense of accomplishment and competence. This is certainly a key ingredient of student empowerment. Though separate from the power gained by mastering or controlling something yourself (*power over* a choice, a decision, a behavior, or other outcome) and contributing to shared power (*power with*), this inner power is fueled by both the other kinds of power. Plan intentional practices to regularly build this inner power for students:

- Discuss with students the concept of power within themselves. Take some time each day or week for students to identify and share successes at reaching high expectations and meeting challenges (academic or behavioral).
- Encourage students to describe what these successes mean to them—how the successes affect them personally, how they increase competence, self-worth, or growth. This can be done in journals or through sharing with a peer or small group.
- Help students see their growing power within as a springboard for greater empowerment. They can reflect on what an increased sense of capability (with a speaking skill, for example) enables them to do that they couldn't do before.

A teacher colleague shared this story with us: *From the start of 6th grade, it was clear Pete was struggling. He had frequent tantrums, often during class transitions or when faced with academic challenges such as completing an assignment. These disrupted both his learning and his classmates' and often ended with Pete being overwhelmed, storming out, and collapsing in the hallway. This pattern repeated itself almost every day, disrupting the flow of his day and reinforcing a negative cycle of behavior.*

A comprehensive evaluation revealed that Pete was on the autism spectrum, leading to new support focused on social communication and learning strategies. Gradually, he began to engage more, though progress came slowly.

A bright spot emerged when Pete became interested in working in the student store managed by his special education teacher. Despite the challenges he faced in the classroom, he was a reliable and responsible worker. He arrived early, worked well with other staff members, and provided excellent customer service to his peers. His dedication and positive contributions at the student store became one of the few successes in an otherwise difficult 6th-grade year. But in 7th grade, as academic expectations rose, Pete's old patterns resurfaced.

One day, after being handed a math worksheet, he crumpled it and threw it across the room. His teacher stayed calm, knelt beside him, and asked, "Do you like working at the student store?" Pete immediately said yes. "Good," she replied. "I like it when you work and learn at school. From now on, you can earn extra store time." She explained that completing assignments in any class would earn him minutes to spend on store projects—reorganizing shelves, making posters, or designing displays. Together, they agreed with his suggestion that one completed assignment equals one store minute.

Just four days later, Pete proudly announced, "I've done more work this week than in all of 6th grade!" The plan wasn't perfect, and he still faced challenges, but it marked a turning point. For the first time, he recognized that something he valued was directly influenced by his academic and behavioral efforts.

Before long, he was promoted to "assistant manager." Being trusted in this role empowered him, as it was the first time he had been genuinely "in charge" of something. That sense of responsibility gave him pride in his work and a new glimpse of his own potential. This, in turn, began to positively influence his academic efforts and lead to stronger self-regulation of his behavior.

CHAPTER 12

EMPOWER Students with Meaningful Learning

In the mid to late 1980s, the Pacific Northwest was embroiled in the spotted owl controversy that pitted individual loggers and sawmill owners against environmentalists. Timber harvests were being reduced, leading to a decreased supply of lumber with higher prices. Jobs were declining, and loggers were losing their means of making a living. Environmental groups were pushing for the spotted owl to become an endangered species. The controversy appeared on TV and in newspapers, magazines, and other media. Students at my (Patti's) school located in southern Oregon were aware of the situation, especially since many families made their living in the timber industry.

I happened to have a fabulous student teacher (we hired her the next year!) who came up with a simulation based on this controversy. Our 6th-grade students were randomly divided into two groups—the loggers and the environmentalists. She told students that while their personal opinions were valued and could be shared later as they felt comfortable, for the purposes of the simulation, they were going to argue from an assigned point of view, whether that was their own or the opposite of their own.

The assignment: The county commissioners (played by five teachers in the building) were holding a hearing to determine the fate of a 150-acre plot of timber land. Should it be given protected status, or should logging be allowed on it? Each group had to research the issue from their assigned viewpoint and be prepared to give a fifteen-minute presentation to the commission and answer any questions they may have. Additionally, after both presentations were complete, each group was given the opportunity to offer a three-minute rebuttal to the other group's presentation.

I honestly don't remember which side "won" the argument, but I do remember students being very excited on presentation day. They were prepared, and some even dressed the part (completely stereotyped) with logging hats, boots, and suspenders in one group and tie-dyed clothes, bell bottoms, and sandals in the other.

Overall, students were empowered by learning, collaborating, and practicing skills based on a real-life situation, one that was impacting the entire state of Oregon and was regularly being discussed everywhere, including as a featured topic in the May 1990 issue of Life magazine.[1]

According to psychologist David Ausubel, who developed the concept of *meaningful learning,* learning is meaningful when new information connects to what learners already know or have experienced, fitting it into their existing cognitive structure. They associate something new with knowledge and experiences that are valuable to them emotionally, ones that resonate and have a personal significance and purpose to them. This personal association empowers students to take ownership of their learning Teachers can promote meaningful learning by designing instruction that is relevant, connected to prior knowledge, engaging, reflective, and applicable to real-life situations.[2]

Put It Into Practice

Implement Practices that Promote Meaningful Learning

There are many experiences and instructional practices that empower students by deepening meaningful learning in the classroom. Here are some tested actions:[3]

+ Guide students in connecting previous learning to new learning. Students don't always make that leap on their own. Start lessons with an activating strategy or a hook designed to connect prior knowledge to new learnings. Use real-world problems, intriguing questions, short videos, props, pop culture references, or surprising statements designed to grab attention and create curiosity. Keep it short, and be sure it makes a valid connection. In a lesson that's focusing on understanding how air masses impact the weather, you might start out by saying, *Think back to last week when it was sunny in the morning, but by lunchtime it was pouring down rain. What do you think might have caused that to happen?* The purpose is to make students eager to learn the new content by connecting it to their existing knowledge or interests. (See Chapter 3 for more about learning transfer.)

+ Identify misconceptions that need to be corrected and gaps that must be bridged between what is known and what needs to be known. Doing this gives students the foundation of understanding upon which they can build connections to new content. They can see how what they are learning fits to what they now know.

+ Assess what your students know. Brainstorm about the topic or concept to be studied. For example, write *plate tectonics* on the board, and ask students to write down or tell you everything they know about it. This will give you an idea of what is known and show misconceptions students may already have. It will give you a good starting point to fill in gaps and continue with new learning. Try using a K-W-L chart where students write and categorize what they already know about a topic (in the K column) and then write a question or two about what they want to know (in the W column). After the lesson, they write what they learned in the L column. (See Chapter 8 for suggestions of ways to assess prior knowledge.)

- Help students continually expand their foundation of knowledge and experiences to build meaningful understanding and connect new ideas. Students with wide and varied experiences can more easily connect classroom topics to what they already know. Students with limited experiences often struggle to make these connections, making it harder for them to find meaning in new learning. Work with colleagues to develop plans and tools that strengthen students' prior knowledge in your subject. Pre-teach key concepts and vocabulary and gather hands-on materials, real-life examples, and multimedia resources to introduce upcoming content.

- Pay attention to the attributes of meaningful learning: That is, when introducing new material, design learning that connects to what students already know or have lived, carries personal or emotional value, resonates with their interests, or has a clear purpose they can understand. When teaching about electricity, a 3rd-grade teacher gives students materials and guidance to build a simple circuit. In the next lesson, they extend their learning by adding a small lightbulb, applying their understanding to a new situation.

- As you teach, craft questions and short activities that will trigger students' critical thinking and lead to connections that will help them learn the new content (even if they don't have much previous knowledge that seems applicable):

- Primary students may not recognize the word *gravity* or think they know anything about it. You can ask, *Have you ever thrown a ball in the air? What happens to it after you throw it? Why?* This triggers students to analyze the situation and infer a cause about why the ball falls to the ground.
- When approaching the topic of idioms and metaphors, students may not know those terms or be able to describe their meaning; but in their lives, they have probably heard someone say, *It's raining cats and dogs,* or *Your room looks like the aftermath of a tornado.* Their brains have to imagine cats and dogs falling from the sky or remember the pictures they've seen of tornado damage and translate those images to the literal concepts of a deluge of rain or a massive mess in the bedroom. This takes creative thinking and knowledge transfer.
- Students can use the knowledge that a submarine operates under the water to help understand the meaning of a new vocabulary word *substandard.* When they do this, they draw on previous understanding of the concept of *sub* and combine it with their previous understanding of *standard* to "get" the meaning of the new word. Using prior knowledge to make sense of new learning is one of the primary stages of critical thinking.

Champion Relevance

Relevance plays a crucial role in effective and meaningful learning and is one of the strongest factors in promoting student empowerment, engagement, and intrinsic motivation. While relevance may appear similar to meaningful learning, it is not the same thing. Relevance itself is not learning; rather, it describes the quality of something that connects with the learner in a way that can influence learning outcomes, thus helping to make learning meaningful.

Researchers Stacy Pinski, Caeron Hecht, and Judith Harackiewicz describe *relevance* as *personal meaningfulness*, how much a person feels that something relates to them personally.[4] For something to be truly relevant, it has to both connect with the learner and matter personally in some way. That "something" could be anything, such as a topic, an experience, an idea, an object, or even a presentation. Here are some actions that infuse the empowering ingredient of relevance into the experiences you provide for students:

- Establish relevance for learning (concepts, tasks, assignments, projects, expectations). Students often ask, *When will I ever use this?* or *Why do we have to learn this?* They want to understand how the content they're learning connects to their lives. When students can see a clear reason for learning something, they're more likely to care about it and put in real effort. When learning feels relevant, students engage on several levels:
  - **Thinking (cognitive):** They're curious and eager to master new skills.
  - **Doing (behavioral):** They take part, work with others, stay focused, and keep trying.
  - **Feeling (emotional):** They feel connected, capable, and proud of their progress.

If students don't see the point of a lesson, it's harder for them to learn, remember, or use what they've been taught. As much as possible, teachers need to build relevance by designing lessons that connect to students' personal interests and real-life situations. Research by David Kember, Amber Ho, and Celina Hong found that relevance is one of the strongest motivators for learning.[6] We empower students to dig deeper into their learning when they can see how a topic relates to their own lives and the world around them.

To help students find meaning, teachers can encourage them to think about such questions as:

- *Why is this worth learning?*
- *How does it work in the real world?*
- *How does it connect to what I already know?*

When students understand the purpose behind their learning, their motivation grows, their curiosity deepens, and the knowledge sticks with them beyond the classroom.

- Understand different kinds of relevance. Different experiences or topics connect with students at different levels of personal meaning and stimulate relevance in different ways. Pinski, Hecht, and Harackiewicz describe a continuum of three types of personal relevance, each one more complex than the other. As a continuum, each kind is a base for the next, and the subsequent kinds of relevance won't develop without the earlier ones:
  - *Personal Association* happens when students connect what they're learning to a past experience or memory. A student solving a math problem about the height of a tree might recall when a tree fell at home in the yard or when she saw an eagle's nest high up in a tall tree or when she climbed too high in a tree. The height of the tree or figuring that out might not be all that important to her; the connection comes from the memory. This is the **least powerful** kind of relevance.
  - *Personal Usefulness* occurs when students see how what they're learning can help them reach a personal goal. A football player might study the team playbook carefully because

he wants to play well and help his team win. A student might learn graphic design to improve her project, website, or Instagram posts, seek out information about 1st Amendment protections so she knows what everyone is talking about in the news, or work hard to improve reading so she's not embarrassed when reading aloud. Another might want to learn about muscles so she knows how to lift weights properly. This type of relevance is **stronger,** because the learning feels practical and helpful.

- *Identification* is the **strongest** type of relevance. It happens when learning connects to who a student is or wants to become. A student who dreams of being a software designer finds technology projects deeply meaningful because they fit her identity and future goals for herself. Another student finds assignments for writing informational texts relevant because he envisions himself as a news correspondent traveling to the far reaches of the globe. A student who identifies as a math nerd wants to learn everything he possibly can about complex problem-solving.[5]

The types of personal relevance are not mutually exclusive. The football player may be stimulated to avidly study that playbook out of personal usefulness, but the relevance of that learning may also be connected to personal association of the great times he had with his brothers playing tag football when they were very young. Also, students move among these types of relevance depending on the task or context, and what feels personally meaningful can change over time. Recognizing these types of relevance helps teachers design experiences that connect meaningfully to students' lives, goals, and self-concepts.

- Build relevance in your lessons. Focus on connecting learning to students' lives, goals, and the world around them:

- **Know your students.** Learn about their interests, backgrounds, and experiences so you can connect lessons to what matters to them.
- **Show the purpose.** Help students see how their work relates to current events, social influences, or community needs. Talk with students about how what they're learning applies now and in the future, especially in subjects where that connection isn't obvious.
- **Honor voice and choice.** Give students options in how they learn or show what they know. Let them connect assignments to personal interests while still meeting learning goals.
- **Use technology wisely.** Incorporate digital tools and platforms to enhance empowerment and autonomy, but balance them with meaningful, hands-on learning.
- **Create or use authentic audiences.** To show real-world impact, give students opportunities to share their work with others through presentations, community projects, or digital publishing.
- **Make cross-subject connections.** Highlight how different subjects overlap. Ask students, *How does math support design? How does science connect to music?*
- **Encourage reflection.** Have students regularly think about what they learned, why it matters, and how it helps them grow.

Look Beyond the Standards

As mentioned earlier, meaningful learning occurs when new ideas connect to what students already know or to experiences that matter personally, giving the learning emotional resonance, purpose, and significance. This level of learning is not only about connecting new concepts to students' lives but also about helping them engage with the world. As a result, engaging students in powerful learning can (and should) extend far beyond meeting academic standards. While our book focuses on helping students master content standards, we would be remiss not to acknowledge that some of the most significant learning in schools isn't directly tied to academic standards. Schools also play an essential role in fostering students' personal development by promoting their social, emotional, and civic growth.

> Meaningful learning occurs when new ideas connect to what students already know or to experiences that matter personally, giving the learning emotional resonance, purpose, and significance.

As we empower students to have more control over their learning, it should extend outward to real social and community issues and cultivate both deep understanding and a sense of responsibility toward others. We're sure that many of you have been approached by students eager to support struggling families, address community needs, or even respond to global crises. When students are empowered to look beyond themselves, they develop a broader awareness and compassion as well as the attitudes and skills that foster respect, tolerance, and inclusion.

But the question becomes, how do we find time to do this? When possible, connect these student-driven projects to academic standards through research, writing, data analysis, or content-area applications so students meet learning goals while exploring issues they care about. If students want to support a local animal shelter, they can research its needs, analyze donation data, and write persuasive letters, all of which reinforce academic skills while engaging in meaningful learning that helps them feel empowered.

Short, structured opportunities such as advisory periods, homerooms, class meetings, project blocks, or clubs can also nurture empathy and awareness without taking significant time from core instruction. Additionally, these can take place in after-school or weekend hours. By empowering students to choose meaningful causes and situations and supporting them in bringing their ideas to life, academic learning becomes more relevant, engaging, and authentic. Here are a few ideas that have been implemented in schools where we have worked or visited:

- Volunteer, as age-appropriate, with libraries, animal shelters, community gardens, food banks, soup kitchens, homeless shelters, museums, disaster response teams, and other local programs.
- Participate in neighborhood cleanups, tree-planting days, town parades, and community events. Host a "fun run" to support a cause.
- Collect and help distribute clothing, food, books, sports equipment, and electronics.
- Gather supplies for schools and youth programs. Hold a penny war to raise money for a cause. A penny in your class jar is worth one point; a dime put in another class jar is worth ten points.
- Visit a local nursing home to sing, chat with residents, or share treats.
- Engage civically by writing to newspapers or legislators, presenting to the school board, or raising awareness about issues like poverty, health, and safety.
- Host a senior citizen night at school. Invite grandparents, older neighbors, and residents of senior homes to learn about technology, create art, dance with students, enjoy a cakewalk, or have their blood pressure checked by the school nurse.

It's important to remember that powerful learning in schools isn't limited to what standards measure; it comes from experiences that resonate with students' lives, identities, and emotions. Meaningful learning, therefore, includes, but can also surpass, mastering content standards. It recognizes that powerful, lasting learning grows from personal relevance and authentic experiences, not just meeting benchmarks.

I've (Laurie) shared this story many times, but it still inspires me every spring. For more than a decade, our district has hosted a student-led school board work session, the culminating event in our 4th- and 8th-graders' persuasive writing and speaking units. Students research, draft, and refine persuasive essays and then work alongside teachers, peers, and adult volunteer writing coaches to polish their writing and prepare to present their persuasive essays as speeches before a public audience.

Each 4th and 8th grader presents to classmates, who choose ten finalists per grade to deliver their speeches to the school board, teachers, families, and community members. It's reminiscent of a youth TED Talk. Watching these students, often nervous but passionate, advocate for meaningful change before an authentic audience never fails to move me.

Over the years, their proposals have sparked real action: a new district pavilion, cross- country for K–8, more drinking fountains, flexible seating, dry-erase desks, hands-free hall passes, new athletic uniforms, cafeteria microwaves, an American Sign Language club, better locker-room hygiene, adding lights to flagpoles, placing soccer nets on goals, and many other great ideas (some of which I can't believe we didn't think of ourselves).

Students walk away having mastered academic skills that matter—researching, reasoning, writing, and presenting with purpose. And I walk away reminded that when young voices are heard, incredible things can happen.

EMPOWER Students with Challenge and Success

When I (Patti) was growing up, it's fair to say I wasn't athletically inclined. Overweight and clumsy, I was always one of the last picked for teams. I managed to get through PE in elementary school and had an understanding teacher in junior high who recognized effort. But then came 9th grade and a PE teacher new to both the profession and the school. After each unit, she called us in to receive our grade based on performance. I still remember her telling me there must have been one event I could do well in during track and field, "but no, not even in shot put or discus." This was a disheartening evaluation, but the real blow came after gymnastics.

We were expected to show skill in all areas—balance beam, uneven bars, vault, and floor exercise. I worked hard to master a backward somersault on the balance beam, albeit set only a few inches off the floor. With friends spotting me, I was successful and felt proud of myself. I managed a few moves for floor exercise but was pretty much a failure on the uneven bars and the vault. So, I steeled myself when it was time for the dreaded conference, but I did feel I'd done well in at least one area. When I met with her, she dismissed all of it: "I'm giving you a D, and that's a gift. You never put any *effort into this unit." Not a word about my one accomplishment. I decided then I'd never take another PE class unless required, and I didn't.*

That experience stuck with me. I pushed myself academically but avoided anything physical for fear of failing again. Eventually I realized that mindset was holding me back. I learned to challenge myself physically in new ways. I have since snorkeled in the Galapagos, zip-lined in Costa Rica, and hiked in Machu Picchu.

I've come to understand that challenge is essential for growth, but it should come in a way that encourages and empowers improvement, not in a way that leads to students giving up.

Challenge is for every student, certainly not only for those we might see as advanced. When we provide challenging experiences for students, we automatically let them know we believe in them, that we know they have the power to meet the challenge, that we think they are capable of meeting high standards. When we remove the challenge by offering something too simple, we lower belief and expectations. It is the challenge that encourages students to look ahead, awaken their own curiosity, dig deeper, and become more resilient, all of which are empowering.

> When we provide challenging experiences for students, we automatically let them know we believe in them, that we know they have the power to meet the challenge, that we think they are capable of meeting high standards.

Put It Into Practice

Inspire students with challenge

Students feel more competent and more in control when they accomplish a challenging task (academic or otherwise). When the challenges are appropriate (meaningful, relevant, and just beyond their current abilities but still achievable with effort and support), students have the best chance of taking the risk and meeting higher goals. And nothing empowers students quite like succeeding with a demanding task. Educational psychologist Lev Vygotsky (father of the scaffolding concept) called this area between what students know or can do independently and what they can master (with help) the *Zone of Proximal Development.* According to him, cognitive abilities increase significantly with such tasks.[1] Discuss the following concepts with students; awareness of these will expand their understanding of what they gain from appropriate challenges:

- Teach students about *productive struggle.* This shows that challenge is at the heart of meaningful learning and student empowerment. This concept describes a learning approach defined as follows: "Students grapple with and solve a question or problem that is just beyond their current level of understanding and it requires them to examine multiple avenues of thought. Students wrestle with ideas yet persevere and come up with solutions themselves."[2] Once students know about this concept, they can watch it in action. Let them identify and discuss situations where they see this happening.
- Review the idea of a growth mindset. (See Chapter 2.) Help students understand that, with a growth mindset, they will learn more and come to openly welcome challenges and failures as opportunities to improve and grow.

* Remind students that their brains can grow in capacity and agility. Explain *neuroplasticity*—the brain's ability to change and rewire itself in response to new experiences. The brain actually changes physically to form new pathways and connections among brain cells in response to new experiences. These changes are triggered and strengthened by learning conditions such as sustained emotional and cognitive engagement, regular reflection, frequent spaced repetition (practicing/reviewing a concept after short intervals), and experiences that involve multiple senses.

* Plan hands-on activities allowing students to explore their own mindset, compare fixed and growth mindsets in their own experience, and discover ways to replace a fixed mindset with a growth mindset. They can make charts to identify a situation and describe side-by-side how they could have approached it with a fixed mindset and could change their mindset to one of growth. (Fixed: *I already know all about the geography of the United States.* Growth: *There is much more I can learn about this topic. I can learn the causes behind some of the facts and features that I've learned about before.* Fixed: *I can't possibly climb that rope in PE class.* Growth: *If I can learn some techniques for climbing and do some extra arm-strengthening exercises, I think I can make progress on that challenge.*)

* Teach and discuss the concept of *attribution theory*, the study of perceived causes of success and failures.[3]

  * We tend to attribute our successes and failures to four main causes: the effort we expend, the difficulty of the task, innate ability, and luck (both good and bad). Students of all ages (and even adults) who believe they put in sufficient effort but did not achieve the expected outcome tend to attribute their failure to task difficulty, lack of ability, or bad luck.

- Explain to students that *innate abilities* are talents or capacities we're born with shaped by genetics, biology, or fundamental aspects of how our brains and bodies develop. Because of those factors, there are limits to how much they can be changed through effort or practice. For example, Patti can never be a coloratura soprano no matter how hard she tries (OK, Laurie can't either). While you can't entirely transform your innate capacities, you can maximize your potential within them. The key is to focus effort not on changing what can't be changed, but on developing what can.
- Keep reminding students that they can learn and grow beyond their current level. Encourage them to recognize moments when challenges or failures arise as opportunities to seek help and try new strategies. Reinforce this by pointing out specific examples of how they've learned, stretched, struggled, and then succeeded. Every student has had more experiences with "getting smarter than they realize."

- Teach students about *academic tenacity*, the ability to look beyond short-term concerns to long-term or higher goals and withstand challenges and setbacks to keep moving toward goals. Carol Dweck and her colleagues define it for kids as "working hard and working smart, for a long time."[4] Tenacity is built on strong, respectful relationships in the classroom, guided empowerment with consistent messages of "you are capable of this," and lots of practice and acknowledgement for every indication of taking on challenges and pushing ahead through difficulties. Here are some strategies that are known to help students develop tenacity:
  - Teaching and demonstrating growth mindset; explaining neuroplasticity, with students identifying examples of brain growth that they notice (see above)

- Intentional planning of activities and dialogues to sustain belonging (see Chapter 6)
- Reinforcing an attitude that failure is an opportunity to learn
- Teaching skills of self-reflection and practicing this regularly (see Chapter 14)
- Giving students chances for do-overs
- Setting structures with students for self-monitoring of work or behavior
- Demonstrating concrete behaviors they can use to get around obstacles or try again after a setback

Laurie once had the opportunity to facilitate a panel that included Dr. Dweck. Dweck emphasized the importance of discussing this with students. Their understanding of growth mindset and tenacity can help them see that it is worthwhile to work at developing these skills. Students who expand the combination of growth mindset and academic tenacity will be empowered.

Energize Students with Success

Success fuels motivation and leads to more success but only when that success comes from ventures meaningful to the student and challenging enough to be of value. The process of recognizing, stating, and identifying the value of successes empowers students:

- Have students describe their successes by restating the learning target, sharing the outcome, and explaining what they did to reach it. Emphasize that success isn't just the final result; small milestones matter, too. As students track progress, check off steps, and reflect, they experience the dopamine boost that fuels motivation. Celebrate these small wins, and encourage reflection on the strategies that led to success. This growing sense of competence empowers and strengthens both motivation and commitment. Reinforce it by repeatedly helping students build success in small steps. Then guide reflection with questions like: *How did you get to this solution? What good choices did you make? What would you do differently next time? What advice would you give others?*

+ Address failure as a partner with success. When tasks are adequately challenging, there are likely to be difficulties, setbacks, and obstacles along the way.

+ Teach students that failure is a very valuable part of learning. Often, we learn more from exposure to failure than we do from repeated success. Take care to use language that does not demonize failure. Saying something like, *Show your hands if you got that one right.* makes failure something to avoid. Instead, say, *Who made a mistake or failed at one of these and was able to find the error and correct it? Let's hear your story!* A math teacher in Laurie's district has a section on the classroom wall labeled "Mistake of the Week . . ." and posts a weekly math problem (without the student's name). Students contribute feedback to understand where the thinking or calculation went wrong and to fix the mistake.

+ Many learners of all ages, levels, and fields have adopted the expression "F.A.I.L.= First Attempt in Learning" for a mindset of viewing failure as an opportunity to learn more.[5] Use this idea as a motto for embracing the reality that failure is a part of learning. It teaches you something about yourself and your learning. There is no negativity or shame connected with it. Tenacity is built through re-learning, re-assessing, and learning again.

+ When we celebrate success, it should not be just about honoring the end product. We must let students know that we celebrate the entire learning process, including the glitches, mess-ups, discouragements, or outright failures. We celebrate the effort and persistence, the lessons learned, the pivotal decisions made, and the pride in getting past the hard stuff.

+ Help students plan ahead for roadblocks. They can be prepared with ways to de-stress and get a break from frustration or a sinking mindset (deep breathing, personal affirmations, visualization, stepping away, getting feedback from a peer or teacher). High school teacher Donna Phillips suggests that her students each keep a "personal playbook" with a refined list of three to five strategies that have helped them get through challenges in the past. She says these "become a confidence anchor" for students when they get overwhelmed.[6]

Incorporate Metacognition Often

Metacognition is the ability to be aware of, reflect on, and guide one's own thinking, a deliberate practice of "thinking about thinking," as it is described by Robin Fogarty and Brian Pete, authors of *Megacognition: The Neglected Skill Set for Empowering Students*.[7] A set of abilities for knowing what you think and how you think, it involves higher-order processes that deepen understanding, analysis, and control over learning. Metacognition is strongly linked to academic success and key skills like communication, collaboration, self-awareness, self-regulation, and resilience. It empowers students to take ownership of their learning, leading to greater achievement and deeper insight into themselves and the world around them.[8]

+ Recognize metacognition when you see it. Teach students to do the same. They are using metacognition when they:
  - Set goals and make a plan for learning: Re-stating goals, identifying needed skills, and developing steps to achieve them.

- Monitor progress using self-questioning or checklists: Pausing to assess where they are, what's working, and what adjustments are needed.
- Use cognitive analysis to notice or plan processes they used or will use for a task: Identifying thinking skills, planning skills, and organizational processes that were used or will be needed.
- Reflect on their performance and evaluate the effectiveness of their thinking and learning: Analyzing what worked, what didn't, and what strategies to use next time.
- Select and apply specific strategies to meet learning goals: Consciously choosing and adapting strategies or tools based on task demands.
- Apply previous knowledge and experience to new tasks or situations: Encouraging transfer of learning and recognizing patterns across contexts.
- Think out loud (verbalize thinking): Making thinking visible, supporting self-awareness and modeling problem-solving processes. Make a map, diagram, drawing, outline, list of steps, model, or other form that can be seen to explain your thinking and make it concrete to listeners and yourself.
- Engage in thoughtful discussions and experience of interdependence that is part of collaboration with peers: Listening, questioning, summarizing, negotiating, and reflecting on multiple perspectives. (See Chapter 7 for more on peer collaboration and interdependence.)
- Ask and answer cognitively challenging, open-ended questions: Promoting deeper inquiry, self-reflection, and critical thinking about learning.
- Predict future performance: Making a judgment about how well they will do on an upcoming test or assignment. Students look over the material they are expected to know and

consider how well they understand the concepts or have mastered the skills. Given their conclusions, they predict how they will perform. For students who are not completely confident that they know exactly what to do and will do well, they ask, *What would I need to do in order to ace this test or assignment?* Answers to that question might be: *I need to review the steps in the problem. I need to understand the meaning of these terms. I am unclear on these two concepts. I need to get some help understanding them. I need to make a study guide. I need to clarify what the key points are. I need to read that chapter I skipped.* From those insights, students can make a plan to prepare for the test or work on the assignment. Generally, this process leads to performances greater than they predicted. John Hattie's research to identify practices that influence learning positively found self-reported (predicted) grades as one of the highest rated effects on student performance and achievement.[9]

- Teach metacognitive skills (such as those mentioned in the section above) in the context of planned lessons and content; don't add to the curriculum. Use a variety of approaches: teacher modeling, role-playing, peer modeling, teacher-student or peer conferences about a specific assignment or project, and feedback sessions. Help students learn and practice metacognition:
  - Define and explain *metacognition* explicitly. Teach what it is, why it matters, and how it supports learning. Invite student examples where students point out when metacognition is being used or is needed (noticing when rereading is needed, where reflection helped improve a product, or where the learning required them to adapt previous learning to a new situation).
  - Know your content, and plan purposeful metacognitive opportunities. Strong content knowledge supports lessons

that promote higher-order thinking. Plan questions and tasks that ask students to anticipate, act, and reflect.

- Observe students, and reflect on your own thinking as you do this. Be aware of your thought processes, and notice how students make decisions, solve problems, and self-correct.
- Model your thinking aloud. Talk through your cognitive steps before, during, and after tasks, showing how you plan, monitor, and evaluate your work.
- When students are taking a strong hand in designing a learning task, ask them to include these phases:
  - **Planning:** *What do I know? What do I need to do? What have I used in the past that I can put to use here?*
  - **Monitoring:** *How am I doing? Are my strategies working? What needs to change?*
  - **Evaluating:** *What worked? Why did it work? What will I do differently next time?*
- Ask open-ended questions. Encourage students to talk about their thinking. Foster dialogue that values curiosity, reflection, and flexible thinking. Encourage reflection and deeper thinking with prompts. Students can record reflections using learning logs or journals in written, drawn, digital, or audio formats with simple prompts. Consider asking these questions: *What challenges did you encounter? How did you respond to them? How did you feel about the lesson before you began? How did that affect the way you learned? How actively engaged and committed to your learning are you today?*

Achieving Content Extensions (ACE) is our (Laurie's) district's Gifted and Talented Program. It provides students with opportunities to extend their learning beyond the general education classroom experience. Beginning each September, participating students (including those who show interest, even if they don't meet formal criteria) meet weekly after school to explore topics and projects that challenge and inspire them. Many students balance ACE with other commitments such as sports and clubs, and the program's flexible structure allows them to participate as their schedules permit, one of the reasons students continue to return year after year.

Over the years, students have presented projects on topics ranging from Legos, building truss bridges, Minecraft, circuit boards, coding, robotics, geodes, Gravitrax, and engineering and physics to painting, birds, pirate ships, fluid dynamics, the Revolutionary War, and clay construction.

Through ACE, students engage deeply in their areas of interest and strength while developing higher-level thinking, creativity, and real-world problem-solving skills. Each student designs and completes a passion project or Genius Hour-style project where students explore their own interests and passions. The year culminates with the ACE Expo, where students proudly present their projects—showcasing their knowledge, creativity, and experiences—to board members, staff, students, and families.

These students dedicate their personal time to a program that isn't required simply because they want the challenge of learning more about something that genuinely interests them. They give their time for challenge and learning but also become deeply invested in something important to them. They gain a greater sense of competence and independence and the experience of a completely self-directed accomplishment, all of which are evidence of increased personal empowerment. These kinds of experiences are not limited to programs for advanced students only. We strive to provide many wonderful opportunities within our general education classes for students to pursue projects that excite them.

CHAPTER 14

EMPOWER Students with Self-Reflection and Self-Evaluation

A few years ago, my (Laurie's) K through 8th-grade district implemented a weekly student reflection practice, emphasizing responsibility, self-evaluation, and goal setting. Families are also encouraged to review the reflections, but the core purpose is student reflection and self-evaluation.

Every grade in our preschool through 8th-grade school district participates in weekly reflections. For our youngest learners, this might look like a "Look What I Did This Week" sheet with a photo, a drawing of something they learned, or simple choices like smiley, neutral, or frowny faces for "My Week Was." As students get older, their reflections deepen and respond to prompts like "What's something I need to work on?" or "What was a highlight of my week?"

In our junior high school (that operates on a middle school model), all students use a common reflection form to track absences, tardies, and missing work as well as answer prompts such as "My most successful class this week was...," "The class I need more support in is...," and "My weekly *goal is… ." They end with reflections on their goal progress and level of commitment. Students then take weekly reflections home to families.*

Although it takes a few minutes each week, the results are well worth it. The process strengthens student-family communication and, more importantly, helps students consistently take ownership of their learning, effort, goals, and growth, starting from a very young age.

To empower our students to become self-directed learners, we need to equip them with skills to both reflect on their learning experiences and to assess their own performance.

The integration of self-reflection and self-evaluation forms one of the most empowering skillsets that both students and teachers can develop. These two metacognitive strategies play a powerful role in promoting self-improvement and meaningful learning. Each aspect of these processes, individually or combined, strengthens student agency (capacity to take an active role in and ownership of their own learning), motivation, self-confidence, and overall competence. Together, they are among the strongest influences on achievement.[1]

> To empower our students to become self-directed learners, we need to equip them with skills to both reflect on their learning experiences and to assess their own performance.

Put It Into Practice

Understand Self-Reflection and Self-Evaluation

Self-reflection is the process through which students examine and describe their own learning processes, behaviors, and habits. By thoughtfully considering how they approach tasks, solve problems, and respond to challenges, students more clearly understand their own thinking patterns and learning strategies.

Self-evaluation happens when students assess the quality of their own performance against clear standards or criteria. Through this practice, they gain the power and responsibility to monitor their progress, identify areas for growth, and refine their thinking and learning. Self-evaluation strengthens cognitive self-regulation, the ability to direct and manage one's own thinking.

Teach and Practice Self-Reflection

While self-evaluation is a more structured assessment of performance against specific standards to identify strengths and areas for improvement, self-reflection is more introspective. It requires a personal look at learning experiences, thoughts, and feelings to better understand learning. When we teach students to self-reflect, we help them think deeply about their experiences, describing their thoughts and actions, both academic and personal. It is more than a quick look back; it's a meaningful examination and description of **how** they learn. This deliberate practice empowers students to gain a deeper understanding of themselves, both as learners and individuals, by helping them recognize patterns in their thinking and behavior and see how their choices affect their work, mindset, and outcomes.

For the most effective results, introduce self-reflection gradually, and have students practice it regularly. The goal is to help students notice **what** they did and then move on from that to deeply understanding **how** and **why** they learn or perform the way they do:

- **Explain the purpose.** Begin by helping students understand why self-reflection matters. Explain that reflecting on their thinking, choices, and effort helps them grow as learners, identify effective strategies, and improve their performance over time. After reflecting on a few recent social studies quizzes, a student notices that several wrong answers had to do with her misunderstandings of vocabulary terms. She starts identifying key terms in each lesson and unit of content and searches through the text to get an understanding of the meanings. She makes herself a study guide and asks a peer to discuss the terms with her and find examples from maps, diagrams, and other text sources. Another student, reflecting on a math performance, notices he is getting mixed up when he has to flip the (distance = rate x time) formula to find either rate or time instead of distance. He decides to use the strategy of drawing a diagram (with the known quantities) for each problem, which helps him visualize the problems and use the correct formula.

- **Model reflective thinking.** Show students what reflection looks like. "Think aloud" about a task you've done, a lesson you've planned, or a problem you've solved. Describe your steps, strategies you used, what you found difficult, and what helped you meet your goals. Patti used to share her cooking disasters (and successes) with students! "Yesterday I was baking muffins, and it turned into a disaster. I rushed through the recipe, didn't double check the oven temperature, and ended up burning the whole batch. When I thought back, I realized I had missed several steps and figured out what I would change next time. I would slow down, measure more carefully, and set a timer. I'm sharing this with you so you can see how reflection helped me learn from my mistakes so I can plan better in the future."

- **Provide guiding prompts.** Use sentence starters or questions appropriate for age and subject area. *What challenged me? What processes worked well to help me complete the task? What major question did I get answered today, and how did I find that answer? I learned that I can . . . , What role did I play in the group project today? How did I check answers on the quiz today? Here are some steps I took to* *organize my time today… In what ways did I meet my goal today? What would I like to share with a peer about my work on this?*

- **Connect reflection to learning goals.** Instead of saying, *I did OK,* say, *I met the goal for this task, because I supported my main idea with two examples. I asked for help when I needed it and got my work done on time.* Instead of saying, *I messed up,* say, *I forgot about looking at a specific digit in the number before rounding. Now I know to re-read the directions each time. When the problem is "round to the nearest hundredth," I need to look at the digit to the right of the hundredths place.* These are examples of one of the most successful approaches to descriptive reflection and self-monitoring. Instead of focusing heavily on the quality of the work, students use reflection to examine and comment on decisions they made and the results that came from those decisions. This invites their analysis and internalization of their insights. They will then be able to use these insights productively in the next experience. This kind of reflection is fact-based and avoids invoking ego and anxiety or defensiveness.

- **Provide time and structure.** Reflection needs dedicated time; it's not just a quick "add-on" at the end of a lesson. Build in moments during and after key learning experiences for students to pause, think, and reflect in writing or discussion. In your planning, break learning or work on a task into segments. After introducing a concept and working examples, stop and take a few minutes for students to write or otherwise show what they've learned, and comment on it. Or the reflection can include comments on what's confusing, what needs more explanation, or how the learning applies to something important.

- **Encourage sharing and discussion.** Discussing reflections with a peer or in small groups builds confidence, validates different perspectives, and helps students articulate their thinking more clearly.

- **Give feedback on reflections.** Acknowledge student insights, ask follow-up questions, and model deeper thinking when appropriate. Feedback helps students refine their reflective skills over time. Peer feedback can be helpful as can teacher feedback. But only include peer feedback after students are well-trained in appropriate and helpful feedback. (See Chapter 5 for guidelines.)
- **Revisit and act on reflections.** Help students use their reflections as a springboard for future work by setting specific goals or strategies for improvement based on what they've learned about themselves.

While students naturally reflect, they often lean toward negative thoughts. (*I don't have any friends. I'm not smart enough. No one likes me. My hair looks awful.*) Teaching accurate self-reflection helps them look at all the evidence before forming opinions about themselves, whether academically or personally. Discuss this with students; they'll know what you're talking about. Let them brainstorm some of their common reflection thoughts. Identify those that are negative, and challenge students to replace these with positive reflections.

Provide plenty of reflection practice. Students learn best when they have ample opportunities each day to do so. Practice this casually in small moments or in structured activities. Students will begin to take ownership of the process by creating their own questions for reflections, sharing honest thoughts, and reflecting naturally without needing step-by-step guidance.

Teach and Practice Self-Evaluation

Early in my (Patti) teaching career I remember struggling to assess student work fairly and assign accurate letter grades. Looking back, I realize that my grading was often subjective. I recall creating a large, multi-part assignment worth 100 points and developing my own system for dividing those points: 10 for neatness, 25 for spelling and grammar, 10 for turning it in on time, and so on (though I'd certainly adjust those categories today). When a student's mother told me it was the first time she truly understood how her son's grade was determined, I realized that this approach to rubrics had promise but also needed refinement.

We've made great progress since those days. Evaluation considers **how well** something is done. Effective self-evaluation now relies on students using clear, specific criteria such as those found in rubrics or scoring guides to assess their own work in relation to established standards. Teachers can develop the criteria alone or with students, ensuring that expectations for quality learning are explicit and transparent. Sharing and clearly explaining the rubric before students begin a task allows them to use it as a roadmap for guiding and improving their own performance. The self-evaluation process helps students think critically about the quality of their work and recognize patterns in their learning. Over time, regular self-evaluation fosters independence and a stronger sense of responsibility for their growth and progress. Try these gradual steps for teaching self-evaluation for any task process or product:

+ Create an evaluative rubric. To help students get an initial understanding of how to create and use a rubric, ask the class to create a rubric for judging a pizza. Choose four or five qualities to rate like crust, sauce, cheese, toppings, and taste. Then, ask students to describe what each level of quality looks like in terms of levels or degrees of quality: What makes a pizza excellent, good, fair, or poor? Ask them to be specific. In small groups, have students use their rubrics to rate samples of pizza you provide (or pictures of varied pizzas, if real pizzas aren't an option) and compare their results with other groups. This is an easy activity that helps students of all ages learn the basics of using rubrics for self-evaluation.

+ Extend the application of the rubric lesson above. Once they design and use the pizza rubric, ask them to follow the same sequence to specific content areas and skills they have already learned (giving an argumentative speech, identifying the author's purpose or bias in a story, transferring statistical math data to a graph, following steps in a science inquiry). From creating and using the pizza rubric, they will have familiarity and depth to discuss the elements in the new rubric knowledgeably.

+ Model the self-evaluation process. Guide students through an example assignment, demonstrating how to compare the work to each level of the rubric. Explain your reasoning, and make your scoring process transparent. Show specific examples from the assignment that illustrate why certain scores were given to help students clearly see how evidence from their work connects to each rubric level. When using a rubric to evaluate her descriptive paragraph (of a roller-coaster ride), a third grader thinks to herself: *I kept the main idea of fear and thrill through the whole paragraph. I used six interesting details. I could have put the details in a different order. The way I ordered them might confuse a reader. Oops, one of my details is about the cotton candy I bought after the ride. That didn't add to the description of the ride. I think my score fits the criteria of 3 points instead of the maximum of 4 for the content and organization category.*

+ Practice scoring some samples. Using the same rubric you've introduced, have students, alone or in pairs, evaluate a set of anonymous work samples representing a range of quality from excellent to needs improvement. (Save student work from previous years, borrow samples from fellow teachers, or create some samples with intentional features that will help students identify a range of quality on specific skills. Be sure no information identifying the original author is visible.) After scoring, ask them to explain their reasoning, citing specific evidence to support their ratings. Discuss any differences in scores and interpretations of the criteria. Note: If students are to practice using rubrics, make sure the rubrics are created in student-friendly language.

* Monitor progress. Ask students to use the rubric for quick progress checks during the process and again before the final submission. This gives students timely, specific feedback while they're still in the learning process. This also helps students monitor their progress, identify areas that need improvement, and make informed adjustments.

* Progress to student self-evaluation. Have students score their own work using the rubric and explain the reasoning behind their ratings, identifying specific areas for improvement. Encourage them to give evidence from their work to justify their scores and better understand how their performance aligns with the criteria.

Use Different Formats for Self-Reflection or Self-Evaluation

Design multiple ways for students to reflect on or evaluate their learning. While questions and prompts are helpful, there are many creative ways for students to demonstrate, record, and share their thinking. Offering a variety of formats encourages your students to find methods that best fit their comfort level. As they build the habits of reflecting and evaluating, students will also generate their own ideas for how to express their learning. Students might:

* Confer with a teacher to discuss progress and next steps.
* Participate in a whole-class or small-group discussion.
* Pair up with a partner to discuss feedback on evaluations.
* Answer or create their own reflection questions.
* Review examples of reflections and evaluations from peers or teachers to compare approaches.

- Create visuals such as webs, mind maps, graphs, or diagrams to guide reflection and show learning progress or outcomes. There are many wonderful apps online that do this or offer templates for creating these tools. Get suggestions from colleagues, or consider asking students to design one for the class.
- Track growth with before-and-after comparisons of their work.
- Set a goal; outline steps or milestones that will be part of the work toward the goal. At each milestone, ask how the work so far satisfies that step and is contributing toward the goal. Then measure achievement against those goals.
- Write a letter to themselves summarizing growth and next steps.
- Keep a reflection or evaluation journal to document progress.

Combine Reflection and Evaluation

For the greatest impact on learning, self-reflection and self-evaluation work best when combined. Used together in a thoughtful sequence, these two practices give students the most complete and balanced understanding of their learning journey. Even at young ages, combining reflection and evaluation expands thinking, deepens learning, and supports the components of empowerment, competence, self-awareness, self-regulation, and control over one's learning. We caution you to be on the lookout for an imbalance, though, when combining these two processes. Too often, children of all grade levels are mostly (or solely) focused on judgment and evaluation without spending helpful time analyzing or reflecting. This is often true of their self-feedback as well as any feedback they give to each other. Our society does this all the time, and it's hard to break the habit. Guide students to hone the skills of non-judgmental reflection as described above, where they describe how they thought and the decisions they made and tell how that affected the outcome. Do plenty of this before adding opportunities for evaluation:

+ Use the processes in either order. Exactly when you or students reflect and evaluate depends on the nature of the assignment, the desired outcome, the student's capabilities and readiness, and teacher judgment or preference.

  - When students reflect and then evaluate, they first think deeply about what they did and how they felt before deciding how well they performed. This helps them understand themselves as learners and builds awareness before making any judgments about their work.

  - When students evaluate and then reflect, they first assess their performance using specific criteria and then think about why they earned those results and how they can improve. This sequence encourages them to set goals and focus on growth after the evaluation.

+ Take the next steps. What can students do after reflecting and evaluating? This is the time to apply what they've learned. Students can review their notes or journals, summarize key takeaways, and decide what to carry forward into their next project or assignment. They might set a few goals (specific skills to improve, strategies to keep using, or new approaches to try). Teachers can guide this process by asking questions that help students use what they've discovered about how they learn and think.

+ Reflect and evaluate both formally and informally. Reflect and evaluate regularly during the working process, focusing just on what has been done so far. At the end of an assignment, project, or unit, the reflection and evaluation may be of a more formal nature as you expand and apply them to the whole process. A warning: Don't go overboard and ask for a reflection and/ or evaluation at the end of every learning experience. If these are over-used, they can begin to feel tedious and less useful to students. Be selective, and use the processes judicially when it will have the greatest impact on improving learning. However, that doesn't mean that less formal forms of reflection and evaluation can't be infused into your daily instruction. Ask questions that require students to think about their progress and their learning in a more casual way:

- *Which parts of your work meet the assignment criteria best, and of what are you most proud?*
- *What challenges, obstacles, or confusing parts did you face, and how did you handle them?*
- *Which strategies, habits, or approaches worked well, and which should you use again?*
- *Which skills or areas do you need to strengthen to better meet the criteria next time?*
- *How effectively did you manage your time, focus, and effort throughout the assignment?*
- *How did your mindset, confidence, and emotions affect your progress and results?*
- *Are you on the right track, or do you need to adjust your approach to reach your goals?*
- *What additional steps, help, or resources would support your success?*
- *What did you learn or discover about yourself as a learner through this work?*
- *What patterns do you notice in your work, and how can you use them to improve next time?*

With consistent practice, students will begin to internalize these processes as an essential part of how they learn, not just something they **do**; they will see it as something that empowers who they **become** as thinkers and learners.

+ Put reflection and evaluation in practice with student-led conferences. It is one of the most meaningful, real-life ways to put students' skills of reflection and evaluation into practice. When students closely examine their own work to plan, organize, and lead their own conferences with parents or caregivers, they gain a greater understanding and appreciation of themselves as students, articulate their learning processes and accomplishments, build strong commitment to their learning, and assume responsibility for their learning. The process is empowering and satisfying.

Patti's school first introduced student-led conferences in 2000, and the practice eventually spread across the district to elementary and high schools and is still in practice today. It's one of the most empowering approaches a school, or even a single class, can use. Student-led conferences turn traditional parent-teacher meetings into student-centered experiences where students take responsibility for sharing and discussing their learning progress and future goals with family, a significant adult, or teachers.

Students were assigned a conference facilitator to work with for the three years of middle school. All certified staff (including administrators) helped students prepare and present their conferences. Students organized a portfolio of their work to show evidence of their accomplishments (or lack thereof) and used it to reflect on their strengths and areas for growth. They then set goals and outlined steps to reach them. The conferences took place in a supportive environment where adults listened, asked questions, and gave feedback, while teachers observed from a distance, stepping in only if needed.

We discovered there is not one single formula that works in every situation. A successful program must be custom made to fit the needs of each individual school. There are a multitude of resources available to help schools design their own practice. For more information on student-led conferences, see the book I wrote from my school's experiences with this powerful practice of student self-reflection and self-evaluation: *Fostering Student Accountability through Student-Led Conferences.*[2]

As a student-led conference facilitator in our middle school, I (Patti) asked my group of students to self-reflect on their overall school performance and identify both strengths and areas for improvement. I remember a 7th-grade girl finally deciding on one of her goals: she wanted to improve her attendance! As part of the preparation process, she was asked to decide on three actions she could take in order to meet each goal. Her plan: 1) Eat healthier, 2) Go to bed earlier on school nights, and 3) Get a flu shot. I remember thinking that was pretty impressive reflecting and planning for a 7th grader! While I don't remember the specific numbers of absences she ended up with for the year, when we revisited student goals later in the year, I do remember she was proud that her attendance had improved.

Another time, I remember being rather nervous when monitoring Billy's conference. He was a restless 6th grader who had trouble focusing and preparing. When his father tried to peek at his report card, Billy quickly stopped him and said, "This is my conference. You need to hear me talk about my work before you see that!" He then confidently shared his work, goals, and finally his report card, which reflected what he had already shared. Watching Billy take charge of his learning, express his goals, and clearly discuss his progress and areas for improvement showed just how powerful and motivating student-led conferences can be.

CHAPTER 15

EMPOWER Students with Technology

Acolleague who also sponsors the school's video news club (Flex) shared this story with us: *Ghassan had significant challenges during his elementary school years. As a student on the autism spectrum, he struggled with behavior and social interactions. When he entered middle school, I worked with him for three years, during which time he steadily matured, improved, and learned to better manage his behavior and social skills.*

His passion was space. When he joined the school video news club, he created a space-themed news report for every broadcast. The program was popular with both the student body and the community, and Ghassan quickly developed a following. This is a transcript of his introduction for the last space report as he prepared to move on to his next school:

"Hello everyone, and if you're watching this, thank you. It truly means a lot to me. Today I'm officially signing off my role at Flex. It's quite surreal to say goodbye to something that's been such a big part of my life over these past years. I've learned so much, made

great memories, and met amazing people along the way. What started as a simple school club turned into something much more. Through every meeting and production, I learned how to work hard, stay focused, and be part of a team. Now I'm heading into a new chapter with a new school, a new place, and new experiences. I don't know exactly what's ahead, but I'm ready. I'm taking everything I learned here with me. To my teachers, classmates, and everyone else who supported me, thank you. You've helped me grow and supported me through my ups and downs. That means a lot. Keep making this a place where people feel seen and heard. And thank you, Mr. B, for always being there for me. And to whoever takes over my role, Good luck. You've got this. This is Ghassan, signing off for the last time . . . so long, Flex."

This experience empowered him to develop more self-confidence, gain a true sense of belonging, and develop and demonstrate leadership skills among his peers. This growth translated to improved social interactions and self-regulation.

When I (Patti) was in high school, our class took a field trip to see a "powerful" computer that filled an entire house. Today, far more powerful devices fit easily in our pockets or ears (or on our wrists or fingers). Technology has become an inseparable part of modern life. Computers are everywhere, instantly connecting us across the globe. With just a few taps, we can access limitless information, conduct research, stream media, get assistance on anything from artificial intelligence (AI), and control "smart" TVs and home appliances.

Surrounded by technology from early ages, many of our students are already skilled users, often more so than adults. Technology of all kinds empowers them, providing choices and possibilities for what and how they learn, watch, and explore. However, we must all be aware that algorithms, platforms, apps, AI hallucinations (statistically-drawn information that looks credible but is nonsensical, unreasonable, or completely fake), AI slop (AI generated digital clutter, often of questionable content), and media bias exert a lot of control over what our students view and explore. While the internet and AI have valuable information and experiences to empower students and enhance learning, we cannot overlook the power that these have to influence what students see, do, and think. We must be savvy to use the internet in our classrooms in ways to limit that power and help students use critical thinking to make distinctions and decisions that empower, rather than manipulate, what they learn.

Put It Into Practice

Set the Stage for Technology Use

Given the monumental presence of technology in the lives of our students and the profound necessity for its appropriate use, we must take on roles that inform, protect, and prepare students for the technological world:

- Broaden your concept of technology beyond the internet. The Merriam-Webster Dictionary defines technology as "a machine, piece of equipment, method, etc. that is created by the practical application of scientific knowledge".[1] With digital technology being such a huge part of our lives today, we might think of it in terms of the internet and devices that connect to it. But think of all the equipment and methods that students encounter in their lives inside and outside the classroom: TVs, tablets, laptops, cellphones, watches, computers, cameras, printers, projectors, interactive whiteboards, video games, GPS, simulations, video and audio recording and communicating options, podcasts, virtual reality, adaptive and personalized learning systems, collaboration tools, and all kinds of apps.

+ Ensure all students have access to technological devices, internet connectivity, and training in skills they need to use technology effectively. We should also support efforts in our communities to expand access to families without internet capacity.

+ Teach students to be safe, informed, responsible users of technology, not just for today but for a lifetime of learning and digital citizenship.

+ Serve as a role model and mentor for responsible practices, guiding students to develop habits that are ethical, thoughtful, professional, and safe, all traits that lead to long-term success. Students are watching your use of technology. They see and hear you on your phone (some teachers may use their phones in class even if students aren't allowed to). They may see you speeding or driving slowly through the parking lot in your car. They watch you navigate apps and sites as you project lessons or learning materials. They watch your use of all the machines and devices available for classroom use. Talk through your actions as you use technology. Point out the actions you are taking to be ethical, professional, and safe. And, be careful of personal use in front of students.

Embrace the Multiple Benefits of Technology for Students

We understand and appreciate the support technology offers for autonomous learning–for students and adults. Appropriate use of many technological tools, devices, and methods offer key benefits and valuable uses. Take advantage of the benefits of technology to engage students, improve instruction, and meet learning targets:[2]

+ Promote independence. With developmentally-appropriate technologies, students can learn at their own pace, explore interests, and take charge of their progress using online tools and platforms.

- Boost engagement. Interactive platforms make learning more exciting as students gather, organize, and share ideas.
- Expand access to information. Students can instantly explore a vast range of topics once limited to textbooks, libraries, and classroom videos. With tools like virtual reality, they can experience places (from coral reefs to space) and concepts through simulations. But technology-supplied experiences should be only part of the information students receive. Students are awash in data, information, and images on screens, and too much of this is mind-numbing.
- Encourage collaboration. Digital tools like shared documents, discussion boards, and video conferencing help students connect and work together (with classmates in the same room or students across the globe).
- Enable active learning. Technology supports engaging activities such as gamified lessons, simulations, and virtual field trips.
- Inspire creativity and innovation. Using technology, students can easily design and publish original work (videos, podcasts, art, websites, or apps), building creativity and confidence.
- Foster application to the world outside of school. Students can apply what they learn to problems, experiments, and projects in the wider school community, students' neighborhoods and communities, the post-high school world, and the working world.
- Build critical thinking. Through simulations and data analysis, students learn to test ideas, make decisions, and solve problems effectively.
- Prepare for the future. Using digital tools helps students develop essential skills for college, careers, and lifelong learning. This includes many of the devices listed in the first section of this chapter. Students will also need skills with use of digital workplace suites, team collaboration sites, and knowledge-sharing

platforms, as well as fundamental understanding of AI and data protection.

+ Increase student voice. Technology gives students new ways to express themselves, share opinions, and create meaningful work for real audiences.

Integrate Technology Effectively into Lessons

Technology can make learning more engaging, meaningful, and empowering when used with confidence and clear purpose. It supports students in reaching high standards when it's used to enhance learning and not just to entertain or fill time (what a slippery slope this can be for us all!). Choose technology that clearly adds value and purpose, enhancing learning over that which could be achieved had we not used it. Review your lesson for places where students would gain more understanding from watching, creating, or interacting with others. After studying the civil war, images of what the fighting actually looked like broadens understanding of the extensive loss of life. A real-time virtual tour of geographical features of a region shows just what these look like right now. An online connection with a real astronaut gives students studying space science a chance to ask questions of an expert. Using a timeline-creating or timeline-comparing app helps students see key social shifts happening at the same time as political events in the U.S. during the 1920s.

Before introducing any technology into your lesson, choose tools, apps, or platforms that have a specific use for the lesson. If students will practice using geometric formulas, find an app that helps them solve those kinds of problems. If a goal is for students to understand sequences and interconnections of historical events, locate a good site where students can create timelines:

+ Be confident and prepared.
  - Use tools you understand well enough to guide students confidently. Take time to practice using the tool for each of

the kinds of tasks students will try. (Don't try to learn how to share Google Docs while asking students to share a Google Doc.)

- Start small, maybe with just one feature or activity before planning a tech-heavy lesson.

* Practice before the lesson.

- Try out each step just as students will. This will give you a chance to see what works and what doesn't, rearrange or drop steps, and perhaps come up with better ideas. It saves you from potentially embarrassing moments of stumbling into something inappropriate or awkward and keeps you from leading students into wasted or confusing actions. (Also, you avoid looking unprepared or uninformed about the content and processes.)

- Anticipate where problems might occur, and plan how to handle them. A colleague of ours told us about a notebook she kept, starting with her first year of teaching. The title on the notebook was "Things I will do differently next year or never do again!" She kept a running list of things that went wrong, mistakes she made in teaching, places where kids had problems of misunderstandings, and strategies that fell flat. She added things she substituted to correct the mistakes. You can also ask colleagues of like grade level or subject matter for suggestions.

* Always have a backup plan. Technology can fail. Wi-Fi drops, devices freeze, websites crash. Prepare offline options or printable materials so learning continues smoothly. When Laurie's district fell victim to a cyber-attack, no one had access at school to the internet for a few days. Yet, all teachers continued teaching.

- Identify support. Know who can help (technology staff, a colleague, or a student "tech buddy"), and encourage capable students to respectfully assist others when issues arise.

Empowering students to develop confidence and independence with technology requires knowledgeable, prepared teachers who make technology an effective learning tool and not a classroom frustration or filler. So, be sure to:

> Empowering students to develop confidence and independence with technology requires knowledgeable, prepared teachers who make technology an effective learning tool and not a classroom frustration or filler.

- Start with the "why." Know how the lesson is directly aligned with your learning targets, and have a clear understanding of how the technology supports achieving them.
- Prepare students for success. If needed, review and demonstrate tools and processes with students beforehand.
- Guide the learning. Offer reminders, troubleshoot challenges, and celebrate examples of effective use.
- Reflect. What did the use of technology add that the lesson needed? Creativity? Engagement? Deeper understanding of a concept?

Embrace the Four E's of Technology Use: Engage, Enhance, Extend, and Expand

Technology combined with purpose is powerful for learning. Here are some effective ways to put that power into your instruction:

+ Use technology to **engage** students. Use technology to grab students' attention and spark curiosity. Show something that excites or surprises them and, most importantly, connects directly to the topic they're learning. This might be a short video clip, a series of digital images, a short animation, or part of a documentary or slideshow. When Laurie is sharing with students or staff, she often uses quick videos to capture attention, especially to break up longer segments of information. You can also share an interactive activity (song, quick game, or digital demonstration) that students can join individually on their devices. Whatever you choose, make sure the activity clearly links to the lesson content and helps students become eager to explore more.

  Simply using a device doesn't guarantee engagement. Too much screen time or unfocused tech use can actually reduce attention and retention. Aim for purposeful, balanced integration that truly enhances learning, acknowledging that overreliance can weaken students' focus on real-world and face-to-face experiences. Sometimes, a compelling artifact or intriguing question can engage students even more effectively.

+ Use technology to **enhance** instruction. We want to affirm the value of students being in school and engaging in learning experiences with real live human teachers. Teachers have varied and dynamic ways to enhance learning without technology. So choose to use technology as warranted to make a good lesson even more interactive or meaningful. Digital tools can help deliver part or all of a lesson's content in ways that add something that brings a place, person, situation, or idea to life. Students might follow an online program that explains a concept from a new perspective, or you might project a video, animation, or digital presentation that brings the topic to life.

  Technology also offers varied ways to learn through visuals, sound, movement, and interaction. It can be used to show examples, illustrate ideas, or guide vocabulary and concept practice. Students can interact on a content topic with students in other places. Games and simulations can help learners apply skills in engaging, hands-on ways. Use it only as needed, not as the go-to choice for instruction each day.

- Use technology to **extend** the curriculum. Use technology to expand and deepen learning by helping students apply knowledge in new and creative ways. Students might research topics for short tasks or long-term projects, working individually or in groups. They can use cameras or audio recorders to capture images or sounds that connect to classroom learning. Virtual field trips, online discussions, multimedia resources, games, and simulations can all help students explore topics more deeply.

  Students can also extend learning by creating follow-up projects–artwork, videos, dramatic presentations, or music–that show their understanding of content standards. Apps and online tools can help them reflect on their learning, analyze their progress, and evaluate their work. And, technology gives students powerful ways to share and showcase their work with others.

- Use technology to **expand** potential. When computers were first introduced in schools, we knew they had potential but weren't exactly clear how we could use them. Should we teach students how to program? Word processing showed promise, but it was often slow and awkward, sometimes requiring multiple floppy disks just to write and edit.

Today, AI presents a similar challenge. A recent RAND Corporation survey finds that over 50% of students and teachers now use AI for schoolwork.[3] We know it is valuable, but we're still figuring out the best ways to use it. Yes, it can help teachers tailor lessons to each student's needs, supporting both struggling and advanced learners. One of the best examples we have seen is students using AI to study. Students can upload notes and ask AI to develop multiple types of student guides, quizzes, and comprehensive reviews over very specific topics.

But to use AI wisely, schools must create policies and practices that promote transparency, protect student data, and ensure that its use enhances (rather than replaces) human teaching and creativity. Teachers must also be trained to use AI in ways that enrich, expand, and supplement student learning experiences. A few excellent resources for developing safe, healthy AI policies and for good AI teaching practices are identified in this endnote.[4]

Additionally, a call for vigilance is needed as device use in the classroom continues to expand. The reality is that a large percentage of students, particularly middle- and high-school students, when left unsupervised and without a school culture that helps them develop executive function to avoid the temptation, DO use internet access and school-provided tablets for distraction, to avoid the learning at hand, and in some cases, to "slam" on classmates, parents, teachers, and celebrities.

Find Balance in Use of Technology

Recent studies find that children ages eight to nineteen spend up to eight hours a day (or more) on screens (not including school-related time for in-school use and homework).[5] Other research reveals that 95% of U.S. schools report using technology in the classroom.[6] Add to that the time students spend on-screen doing homework and scrolling social media. When we do the math, we see that today's students spend a huge part of their waking hours on-screen, far more than is recommended by health experts. Information from the American Academy of Pediatrics, Mayo Clinic, the Centers for Disease Control, and other health organizations claims that high screen time for children contributes to infrequent physical activity, obesity, sleep disturbances, symptoms of anxiety and depression, social and emotional withdrawal, aggression, hyperactivity, and disruption of peer socialization.[7] An alarming trend is the increased use by teens of AI chatbots for friendship and advice. Recent news exposes the rise in anxiety, depression, and suicide ideation/attempts/successes connected to the rise in AI chatbots sycophancy (telling users what they want to hear, giving advice affirming behavior, even if it is harmful). For some examples of this news, see information in this endnote.[8]

Limiting screen time yields a number of academic, physical, social, and emotional health benefits, including more sleep, better school involvement and performance, more positive behavior, less anxiety, and more positive social interactions.[9]

While technology is a valuable learning tool, teachers must avoid using it as the primary or sole source of learning in the classroom. For strong learning and overall well-being, students need a healthy balance.[10] In your lesson planning, write the points where technology will be used. Reflect on these plans to see that it is used for a specific way of making learning better. Note where its use is over prevalent. Some skills are best learned away from screens through active, hands-on, face-to-face, or group experiences. While Google Meets and Zoom are certainly more convenient and time effective sometimes, I (Laurie), too, often crave more in-person time with colleagues I often only see online now. I'm missing the personal development that comes from in-person dialogue with fewer time constraints, the insights and nonverbal responses that you catch when you can look around a group as you are talking (or as someone else is talking,) and the camaraderie that comes from a group feeling (as opposed to pictures of individuals popping in and out on the screen). Students miss these, as well, when they learn on screens.

Students also need time for calm reflection, focused thinking, movement, and direct interaction with others. Patti has a relative who teaches at a school that is partly online, partly in person. Casual surveys of students revealed that they are growing weary of so much time using computers and are wanting to be involved in more direct, hands-on learning. Similar surveys across this large district are showing similar results. The key is to use technology purposefully, only when it clearly supports learning goals and adds real value to the lesson. Thoughtful balance helps students grow not just as technology learners but also as whole, well-rounded individuals.

Step up Digital Literacy

Digital literacy is a combination of all the skills associated with using digital technology. It is a broad term, encompassing the mechanics of using tech devices along with all the facets of information literacy, media literacy, digital citizenship, and digital safety. Before students can use technology effectively, they need basic computer knowledge, especially younger students. Although many are familiar with devices and applications, not all have equal experience or skill. Here are some ways to establish the foundation students need:

- Build basic computer skills.
  When using computers in the classroom, check what your students already know, realizing younger students may need more explicit instruction. Then cover the basics they will need with targeted teaching (understanding computer terms and operations, opening, closing, and saving files, using word processors, searching the internet, sending emails, and using collaborative tools like online documents or messaging apps).
- Share useful digital tools.
  - Show students digital tools, apps, and platforms that support learning in your subject area. They might collect data for science experiments, do a virtual dissection, create graphs, maps, or models, or participate in online discussions or group projects.
  - Provide a checklist or guide that can help students learn where to go and how to use these tools effectively.

- Teach information and media literacy. *Information literacy* is a set of critical skills needed to access, analyze, evaluate, and ethically use information from any source. *Media literacy* expands the use of those skills in application to all forms and sources of communication used to transmit messages digitally, electronically or through print, sound, or visuals—with special application to mass media. Both require a combination of research, critical thinking, communication skills, and digital technology skills. Teach students to:
  - Determine the quality, accuracy, and validity of all content from digital sources.
  - Identify organizations and authors behind sources.
  - Examine and evaluate all sources for credibility, viewpoint, and bias.
  - Analyze messages, and identify the author's purpose or intent.
  - Recognize trustworthy evidence, and spot misinformation.
  - Think critically about what they read, watch, and hear.
  - Use reliable information from any format to gain knowledge, create products, solve problems, draw conclusions, and make decisions.

Step Up Digital Citizenship

Digital citizenship means using technology such as the internet, social media, and other platforms or devices safely, responsibly, and respectfully. It involves understanding how our online actions can affect ourselves and others. Teach students that good digital citizens use technology to learn, create, express themselves, and build positive connections. The common thread is respect: Good digital citizens use technology safely, kindly, and wisely. These three reminders will give students an easy-to-remember framework for this topic:

- **Respect yourself.** Encourage students to think about what it means to be their best selves, to think before they post, and to share only content they are proud of, knowing it may be seen by anyone (including future colleges, employers, and organizations they may wish to be a part of one day). One way to address this with students is to gather and discuss (appropriate) real experiences of people who have made mistakes in this area. Getting a picture of the real damage that can result from posting before thinking can be a strong motivator.

- **Respect others.** Teach students to listen to and value different viewpoints and cultures. Communicate kindly and thoughtfully. Do not use rude or harmful language or behavior. Stand up against cyberbullying. Don't share hurtful posts, and avoid supporting them, even by "liking" them. Don't share any personal information about anyone else.

- **Respect digital content.** Give credit to creators, not copying or stealing online work, and using information and media responsibly.

Step Up Digital Safety

Digital safety means using technology in ways that protect yourself and others from harm. An important concept for students (and adults) to learn, understand, and practice is recognizing how their digital actions can affect themselves and others. The first step is learning and recognizing dangers that can appear online, practices like cyberbullying, scams, fake information, predators, and privacy invasion. Being a safe digital citizen helps us all enjoy technology with fewer risks. Teach students these strategies to stay smart and safe:

- The internet is forever. Think before you like, post, share, reply, or act.

- Remember that anything you text or post can be copied, shared, or altered.
- Protect privacy. Don't share images, personal information, or passwords (yours or others').
- Use strong passwords.
- Don't click on suspicious links or open unknown attachments.
- Avoid strangers and risky challenges online. Social media platforms where short videos are created and shared can be very enticing (but dangerous when used inappropriately).
- Talk to an adult if something feels wrong, weird, or scary.
- Block bullies, and never respond to mean messages.
- Drill into your students that making safe choices online equals smart, strong, and respectful digital citizens.

Each month in Laurie's school district, teachers from different schools present at school board meetings to showcase learning and activities happening in their classrooms. Often, they bring students along (the best "show and tell" imaginable) to share authentic examples of their work and learning experiences. Many of these presentations highlight the meaningful ways technology is being integrated into instruction and empowering students.

In one board presentation, some of our 7th- and 8th-grade students from BandLab, an elective class that uses the free music-creation software of the same name, demonstrated how they compose and produce original music. Using computers, digital audio workstations, and both virtual and real instruments, students collaborate or work independently to layer loops and sounds, experiment with artificial intelligence to develop ideas, and record, mix, and produce their own tracks.

At another board meeting, a kindergarten teacher brought kindergartners to share their learning. These five- and six-year-olds confidently and knowledgeably explained how they use iPads to explore coding and robotics and then delighted everyone by demonstrating their robots in action.

Time and again, students at these board meetings show how powerful and impactful technology is when used effectively and for the right purposes.

A Culture of Powerful Learning

Teachers are not the only guides to powerful learning. The classroom is not the only place where we work to help students meet high expectations, deepen engagement, and expand empowerment. The most powerful learning experiences and outcomes result from these three pathways when they are deeply embedded in all corners of the school. This cultivates a culture of powerful learning where students, teachers, leaders, non-teaching staff, coaches, parents, and caregivers all learn and strengthen the same practices of high expectations, student engagement, and student empowerment.

In such a culture, here's what happens: Across the school building and grounds, throughout the wider community, and within every district or school policy, procedure, and communication, everyone is on the same page.

Everyone knows what is meant by high expectations, engagement, and empowerment. Everyone believes these are foundational to powerful learning. And everyone understands the processes that build these cornerstones for students. Teachers and leaders intentionally partake in professional development to offer the instruction and support their students need. Leaders provide a climate and experiences that increase teachers' growth in high expectations, engagement, and empowerment for themselves. Students' families are fully informed about these pathways. All classes, teams, and programs in the school find ways to enlist families and each other in the mission to expand them.

In the end, everyone has the same commitment to powerful learning and understands why these three pathways are important. This collaborative force boosts student confidence and achievement, builds a stronger community, and develops school pride. It shows students how many people are in their corner valuing their hard work toward excellence (high expectations), their personal investment in learning (engagement), and the positive growth of their personal power (empowerment) combined. Such a culture is fundamental to an education that all students deserve and one that all teachers can provide.

Endnotes

Foreword

1. Dweck, C. (2007). *Mindset: The new psychology of success.* (pp. 4-14). Ballantine Books.
2. Center for American Progress. (2014, October 6). *The power of the Pygmalion Effect: Teacher expectations strongly predict college completion.* https://www.americanprogress.org/article/the-power-of-the-pygmalion-effect/ Gershenson, S. (2022, November). *The power or expectations in district and charter schools.* Thomas Fordham Institute. https://fordhaminstitute.org/national/research/the-power-of-expectations-district-charter
3. Visible Learning. (2025). *Visible learning research* (para.1). Corwin Visible Learning. https://www.visiblelearning.com/research
4. Visible Learning. (2018). *Hattie ranking: 252 influences and effect sizes related to student achievement.* https://visible-learning.org/hattie-ranking-influences-effect-sizes-learning-achievement/

Introduction: Destination: Powerful Learning

1. Powerful Learning. (2020, March). *Powerful learning.* https://powerfullearning.com/wp-content/uploads/2020/03/PL-Document-updated-Mar-2020-with-DRAFT-watermark.pdf

PART I Expect!

Introduction

1. Rosenthal, R., & Jacobson, L. (1968). *Pygmalion in the classroom: Teacher expectation and pupils' intellectual development.* Holt, Rinehart and Winston.

2. Busch, B. (2017). *Research every teacher should know: Setting expectations.* The Guardian. https://www.theguardian.com/teacher-network/2017/nov/10/what-every-teacher-should-know-about-expectations

3. Aydin, O, & Ok, A. (2022). A Systematic review on teacher's expectations and classroom behaviors. *International Journal of Curriculum and Instructional Studies, 12*(1), 247-274. https://files.eric.ed.gov/fulltext/EJ1349631.pdf
    Boser, U., Wilhelm, M., & Hanna, R. (2014). *The power of the Pygmalion Effect: Teachers' expectations strongly predict college completion.* Center for American Progress. https://www.americanprogress.org/issues/education-k-12/reports/2014/10/06/96806/the-power-of-the-pygmalion-effect/
    Rubie-Davies, C. M., & Hattie, J. A. (2024). The powerful impact of teacher expectations: A narrative review. *Journal of the Royal Society of New Zealand, 55,* 343-371. doi: 10.1080/03036758.2024.2393296

4. Johnston, O., Wildy, H., & Shand, J. (2021). 'Believe in me and I will too': A study of how teachers' expectations instilled confidence in grade 10 students. *Social Psychology of Education, 24.* 1535-1556. doi.org/10.1007/s11218-021-09668-1
    The New Teacher Project. (2024). *The impacts of teacher expectations on student outcomes: A practitioner's literature review.* TNTP. https://tntp.org/publication/the-impacts-of-teacher-expectations-on-student-outcomes/
    Wang, S., Rubie-Davies, C. M., & Meissel, K. (2018). A systematic review of the teacher expectation literature over the past 30 years. *Educational Research and Evaluation, 24*(3–5), 124–179. doi.org/10.1080/13803611.2018.1548798

5. Aydin, O, & Ok, A. (2022). A Systematic review on teacher's expectations and classroom behaviors. *International Journal of Curriculum and*

Instructional Studies, 12(1), 247-274. https://files.eric.ed.gov/fulltext/EJ1349631.pdf

Rubie-Davies, C. M., & Hattie, J. A. (2024). The powerful impact of teacher expectations: A narrative review. *Journal of the Royal Society of New Zealand, 55,* 343-371. doi: 10.1080/03036758.2024.2393296

Chapter 1, EXPECT Students to Strive for Clear and Appropriate Expectations

1. Rubie-Davies, C. M., Peterson, E. R., Sibley, C. G., & Rosenthal, R. (2015). A teacher expectation intervention: Modelling the practices of high expectation teachers. *Contemporary Educational Psychology, 40,* 72–85. doi.org/10.1016/j.cedpsych.2014.03.003
2. Hattie, J. (2023). *Visible learning: The sequel* (pp. 226, 307-310). Routledge.

Chapter 2, EXPECT Students to Receive High-Quality Teacher Support

1. Whitaker, T. (2012), *What great teachers do differently: 17 things that matter most* (p. 34). Routledge.
2. Johnston, O., Wildy, H., & Shand, J. (2021). 'Believe in me and I will too': A study of how teachers' expectations instilled confidence in grade 10 students. *Social Psychology of Education, 24,* 1535-1556. doi.org/10.1007/s11218-021-09668-1
    Rubie-Davies, C. M. (2006). Teacher expectations and student self-perceptions: Exploring relationships. *Psychology in the Schools, 43,* 537–552. doi.org/10.1002/pits.20169
3. Johnston, O., Wildy, H., & Shand, J. (2021). 'Believe in me and I will too': A study of how teachers' expectations instilled confidence in grade 10 students. (page 1549). *Social Psychology of Education,* (24), 1535-1556. doi.org/10.1007/s11218-021-09668-1
4. Hattie, J. (2023). *Visible learning: The sequel* (p. 226). Routledge.
5. Huang, J. (2025). Research on the role of self-efficacy in educational achievement. *Journal of Education, Humanities and Social Sciences, 59,* 110-117. DOI:10.54097/51p6q931

Weir, K. (2025, October 22). *Self-efficacy: The theory at the heart of human agency*. American Psychological Association. https://www.apa.org/research-practice/conduct-research/self-efficacy-human-agency

6. Dweck, C. (2007). *Mindset: The new psychology of success*, Ballantine Books.

    Stanford Teaching Commons. (2026). *Growth mindset and enhanced learning. Stanford University.* https://teachingcommons.stanford.edu/teaching-guides/foundations-course-design/learning-activities/growth-mindset-and-enhanced-learning

    YouTube. There are several videos by Carol Dweck on growth mindset to be found here. Explore her name and the topic to hear more from her directly.

7. Growth Mindset Institute. (2018). *Growth mindset definition.* https://www.growthmindsetinstitute.org/2018/03/08/growth-and-fixed-mindset-definition/

8. Rubie-Davies, C. (2007). Classroom interactions: Exploring the practices of high- and low-expectation teachers. *British Journal of Educational Psychology 77*(2), 289-306.

    Rubie-Davies, C. (2018) *How to develop high expectations teaching.* The Education Hub.

    https://theeducationhub.org.nz/wp-content/uploads/2018/06/How-to-develop-high-expectations-teaching.pdf

Chapter 3, EXPECT Students to Aim High with Academics

1. Makel, M. C., Matthews, M. S., Peters, S. J., Rambo-Hernandez, K., & Plucker, J. A. (2016, September). *How can so many students be invisible? Large percentages of American students perform above grade level* (pp. 4-10). Johns Hopkins School of Education Institute for Education Policy. https://jscholarship.library.jhu.edu/server/api/core/bitstreams/3ef1a032-2a6a-4c5d-b4da-f13013a1a9fc/content

2. Marshall, J., Fisher, D, Frey, N. (2005, Spring). RIGOR walks: Development and initial validation of a framework to support rigorous learning environments. *Journal of School Administration Research and Development, 10*(1), 3-20.

3.	Anderson, L. W., & Krathwohl, D. R. (Eds). (2001). *A taxonomy for learning, teaching, and Assessing: A revision of Bloom's taxonomy of educational objectives.* Allyn & Bacon.
Main, P. (2023, May 11). *Webb's Depth of Knowledge: The four DOK levels with examples.* Structural Learning. https://www.structural-learning.com/post/webbs-depth-of-knowledge

4.	Perkins, D. N., & Salomon, G. (1999, July). *Transfer of learning* (p. 4). ResearchGate. https://www.researchgate.net/publication/2402396_Transfer_Of_Learning

5.	Perkins, D. N., & Salomon, G. (1999, July). *Transfer of learning* (p. 8). ResearchGate. https://www.researchgate.net/publication/2402396_Transfer_Of_Learning

Chapter 4, EXPECT Students to Succeed with Grade-Level Instruction

1.	The New Teacher Project. (2018, September 25). *The opportunity myth: What students can show us about how school is letting them down—and how to fix it* (pp. 9-14). TNTP. https://tntp.org/publication/the-impacts-of-teacher-expectations-on-student-outcomes/

2.	The New Teacher Project. (2018, September 25). *The opportunity myth: What students can show us about how school is letting them down—and how to fix it* (pp. 9-14). TNTP. https://tntp.org/publication/the-impacts-of-teacher-expectations-on-student-outcomes

3.	Region 87 Education Service Center (2026). *The importance of giving students grade-level work.* https://www.esc7.net/apps/news/article/1839383
The New Teacher Project. (2018). *The opportunity myth: What students can show us about how school is letting them down—and how to fix it.* https://tntp.org/assets/documents/TNTP_The-Opportunity-Myth_Web.pdf

Chapter 5, EXPECT Students to Give and Receive Meaningful Feedback

1.   Hattie, J., & Timperley, H. (2007). The power of feedback. *Review of Educational Research, 77*(1), 81-112. doi.org/10.3102/003465430298487
Henderson, M., Ryan, T., Mahoney, P., Boud, D., Dawson, P., Phillips, M., & Molloy, E. (2019). The usefulness of feedback. *Sage Journals, (22)*3. https://journals.sagepub.com/doi/10.1177/146978741987239
Wisniewski, B., Zieger, K., & Hattie, J. (2020, January 22). The power of feedback revisited: A meta-analysis of educational feedback research. *Frontiers in Psychology.* 10.3389/fpsyg.2019.03087

2.   Greene, N. (17 January, 2025). *Feedback Fridays* (paras. 2, 10, 14.) Edutopia. https://www.edutopia.org/article/soliciting-weekly-student-feedback

PART II Engage!

Introduction

1.   Glossary of Educational Reform. (2016, February 18). *Student engagement.* https://www.edglossary.org/student-engagement/
Millacci, T. S. (2024, November 20). *7 student engagement strategies for improved learning.* Positive Psychology. https://positivepsychology.com/student-engagement/

2.   Avanti. (2022, September 30). *What is student engagement and why is it important?* https://www.my-avanti.com/what-is-student-engagement-and-why-is-it-important/
Hodges, T. (2018, October 25). *School engagement is more than just talk.* Gallup. https://www.gallup.com/education/244022/school-engagement-talk.aspx
Wong, Z. Y., Liem, G. A. D., Chan, M., & Datu, J. A. D. (2024). Student engagement and its association with academic achievement and subjective well-being: A systematic review and meta-analysis. *Journal of Educational Psychology, 116*(1), 48–75. https://doi.org/10.1037/edu0000833

3.   Hodges, T. (2018, October 25). *School engagement is more than just talk.* Gallup. https://www.gallup.com/education/244022/school-engagement-talk.aspx

Lei, H., Cui, Y., & Zhou, W. (2018, March). Relationships between student engagement and academic achievement: A meta-analysis. *Social Behavior and Personality: An International Journal 46*(3), 517-528. DOI:10.2224/sbp.7054

4. Holooquist, S. E., Cetz, J., O'Neil, S. D., Smiley, D., Taylor, L. M., & Crowder, M. K. (2020). *The "silent epidemic" finds its voice: Demystifying how students view engagement in their learning. McREL International.* https://files.eric.ed.gov/fulltext/ED609966.pdf

Hrynowski, Z. (2024, August 21). *K-12 schools struggle to engage Gen Z students.* Gallup. https://news.gallup.com/poll/648896/schools-struggle-engage-gen-students.aspx

5. School of the Future International Academy. (2025, September 10). *The impact of disengagement on student well-being and academic success.* https://www.linkedin.com/pulse/impact-disengagement-student-well-being-academic-success-sofianet-xjr8f

Winthrop, R., Shoukry, Y., & Nitkin, D. (2025, January). *The disengagement gap: Why student engagement isn't what parents expect.* Center for Universal Education. https://www.brookings.edu/wp-content/uploads/2025/01/REPORT_The-Disengagement-Gap_FINAL.pdf

Chapter 6, ENGAGE Students with Belonging

1. Goodenow, C., & Grady, K. E. (1993). The relationship of school belonging and friends' values to academic motivation among urban adolescent students. *Journal of Experimental Education 62*(1), 60-71. DOI:10.1080/00220973.1993.9943831

2. Allen, K., Kern, M. L., Vella-Brodrick, D., Hattie, J., & Waters, L. (2018). What schools need to know about fostering school belonging: A meta-analysis. *Educational Psychology Review, 30*(1), 1–34.

Allen, K. A. (2022, February 9). A deep dive into the benefits of school belonging: A recap of major research findings. *Psychology Today.* https://www.psychologytoday.com/us/blog/sense-belonging/202202/deep-dive-the-benefits-school-belonging

Gillen-O'Neel, C. (2021). Sense of belonging and student outcomes: A meta-analysis. *Child Development, 92*(5), 1675–1690.

Goodenow, C., & Grady, K. E. (1993). The relationship of school belonging and friends' values to academic motivation among urban adolescent students. *The Journal of Experimental Education, 62*(1), 60–71.

3.   Allen, K. (2026). Measurement tools (for belonging). Dr. Kelly Allen. https://www.drkellyallen.com/measurement-tools
New York City Public Schools. (2022) NYC school surveys: Student well-being. Edinstruments. https://edinstruments.org/instruments?-search=&field_air_student_well_being_tax%5B57%5D=57
U.S Department of Education National Center for Education Statistics (2026).ED school climate surveys. https://safesupportivelearning.ed.gov/sites/default/files/EDSCLS_Questionnaires_112017.pdf

4.   Allen, K., Kern, M. L., Vella-Brodrick, D., Hattie, J., & Waters, L. (2018). What schools need to know about fostering school belonging: A meta-analysis. *Educational Psychology Review, 30*(1), 1–34. DOI:10.1007/s10648-016-9389-8
Barron, L., & Kinney, P. (2024) *The successful middle school: A place to belong and become.* Association for Middle Level Education.

5.   Barron, L., & Kinney, P. (2021). *We Belong: 50 strategies to create community and revolutionize classroom management.* Association for Curriculum Supervision and Development.
Barron, L., & Kinney, P. (2024) *The successful Middle School: A Place to Belong and Become.* Association for Middle Level Education.

6.   Brist, R. (2023) *The successful middle school advisory.* Association for Middle Level Education.

Chapter 7, ENGAGE Students with Peer Interaction

1.   Caine, R. N., Caine, G., McClintic, C., & Klimek, K. J. (2016). *12 brain/min learning principles in action* (p. 54). Corwin.

2.   Furrer, C., & Skinner, E. (2003). Sense of relatedness as a factor in children's academic engagement and performance. *Journal of Educational Psychology, 95*(1), 148–162. DOI:10.1037/0022-0663.95.1.148
Shao, Y., Kang, S., Lu, Q. *et al.* (2004). How peer relationships affect academic achievement among junior high school students: The chain mediating roles of learning motivation and learning engagement. *BMC Psychology 12,* 278. doi.org/10.1186/s40359-024-01780-z

3.   Kay, M. R. (2024). *Promoting deep discussions: A teacher's guide to crafting great questions.* Association for Supervision and Curriculum Development.

4.   Berman, S. (1997). *Children's social consciousness and the development of social responsibility.* State University of New York Press.

5.   Berman, S. (1997). *Children's social consciousness and the development of social responsibility.* State University of New York Press.

6.   Drouet, O. C., Lentillion-Kaestner, V., & Margas, N. (2023). Effects of the Jigsaw method on student educational outcomes: systematic review and meta-analyses. *Frontiers in Psychology, 14.* doi.org/10.3389/fpsyg.2023.1216437

7.   Alotaibi, T. A., et. al. (2023, December 22). The benefits of friendships in academic settings: A systematic review and meta-analysis.) *Cureus Journal of Medical Research, 15*(12). doi: 10.7759/cureus.50946
Cambridge International School. (2024, January 9). *Why is socializing important for student growth?* https://tist.school/blog/why-is-socializing-important-for-student-growth

Chapter 8, ENGAGE Students with Compelling Content

1.   Hattie, J. (2023). *Visible learning: The sequel* (pp. 346, 350-352). Routledge.
Van Kesteren, M. T, Krabbendam, L., & Meeter, M. (2018, June 25). Integrating educational knowledge: Reactivation of prior knowledge during educational learning enhances memory integration. *NPJ Science of Learning Journal.* doi: 10.1038/s41539-018-0027-8
Wenk, L. (2917, September 14). *The importance of engaging prior knowledge.* Center for Teaching and Learning. https://sites.hampshire.edu/ctl/2017/09/14/the-importance-of-engaging-prior-knowledge/

2.   Mahler, D., Groschedl, L., & Harmes, U. (2018, November 21). *Does motivation matter? The relationship between teachers' self-efficacy and enthusiasm and students' performance.* PLoS One. https://scihub.st/10.1371/journal.pone.0207252

Zhang, Q. (2014, February 1). *Teaching with enthusiasm: Engaging students, sparking curiosity, and jumpstarting motivation.* National Communication Association. https://www.natcom.org/publications-library/instructors-corner-3-teaching-enthusiasm-engaging-students-sparking-curiosity/

Chapter 9, ENGAGE Students with Active Experiences

1. Center for Innovative Teaching & Learning, Indiana University. (2016). *Active learning.* CITLhttps://citl.indiana.edu/teaching-resources/evidence-based/active-learning.html
   Doolittle, P., Wojak, K., & Walters, A. (2023, September). Defining active learning: A restricted systemic review. *Teaching & Learning Inquiry The ISSOTL Journal.* DOI:10.20343/teachlearninqu.11.25
2. Caine, R.N., & Caine, G. (1990, October). Understanding a brain-based approach to learning and teaching. *Educational Leadership,* 66. https://files.ascd.org/staticfiles/ascd/pdf/journals/ed_lead/el_199010_caine.pdf
3. Caine, R.N., & Caine, G. (1990, October). Understanding a brain-based approach to learning and teaching. *Educational Leadership,* 69. https://files.ascd.org/staticfiles/ascd/pdf/journals/ed_lead/el_199010_caine.pdf
4. Caine, R.N., & Caine, G. (1990, October). Understanding a brain-based approach to learning and teaching. *Educational Leadership,* 67. https://files.ascd.org/staticfiles/ascd/pdf/journals/ed_lead/el_199010_caine.pdf
5. Haidt, J. (2024). *The Anxious generation: How the great rewiring of childhood is causing an epidemic of mental illness.* Penguin Press.
   Lembke, A. (2023). *Dopamine nation: Finding balance in the age of Indulgence.* Dutton.
   Twenge, J. (2018). *iGen: Why today's super-connected kids are growing up less rebellious, more tolerant, less happy—and completely unprepared for adulthood—and what that means for the rest of us.* Atria.
6. Tourist Landmarks. (2026). *Foxfire Museum and Heritage Center.* https://touristlandmarks.com/landmarks-foxfire-museum-and-heritage-center_johnson-city

Chapter 10, ENGAGE Students with Exploration

1. Isaacs, R. (2025, October 3). *Exploratory learning.* Valparaiso University Center for Innovation in Teaching, Assessment, and Learning. https://intra.valpo.edu/cital/exploratory-learning/

2. Koller, K. (2024, December). Integrating exploration as a learning context impacts feelings of empowerment and engagement. *International Journal of Educational Research Open, 7.* doi.org/10.1016/j.ijedro.2024.100374
   Kong, Y. (2021, October 22). *The role of experiential learning on students' motivation and classroom engagement.* National Library of Medicine. doi: 10.3389/fpsyg.2021.771272

3. Kay, M. R. (2024). *Promoting deeper discussions: A teacher's guide to crafting great questions.* Association for Supervision and Curriculum Development.

PART III Empower!

Introduction

1. Broom, C. (2015). Empowering students: Pedagogy that benefits educators and learners. *Citizenship, Social and Economics Education, 14*(2), 79-86. https://doi.org/10.1177/2047173415597142
   Flaherty, A. (2018) Power and empowerment in schools. In Y. Weinberger (Ed.), *Contemporary pedagogies in teacher education and development* (Chapter 2, pp. 23-36). Intech Open. http://dx.doi.org/10.5772/intechopen.76483

2. Broom, C. (2015). Empowering students: Pedagogy that benefits educators and learners. *Citizenship, Social and Economics Education,* (paras. 11-13). https://doi.org/10.1177/2047173415597142

3. Broom, C. (2015). Empowering students: Pedagogy that benefits educators and learners. *Citizenship, Social and Economics Education, 14*(2), 79-86. https://doi.org/10.1177/2047173415597142
   Kirk, C. M., Lewis, R. K., Brown, K., Karibo, B., & Park, E. (2016). The power of student empowerment. *The Journal of Educational Research (109)*6. https://www.jstor.org/stable/26587019

Stelle, J. A. (2026). *Emerging research highlights promise of student empowerment.* Capital Area School Development Association, University at Albany, State University of New York. https://www.casdany.org/student-empowerment

4. Krone, A. D., Sun, C. B., Pasia, L. G., Lopex, I, Ermi, T, & Kohlenberg, B. (2026). *Disempowerment.* Sage Reference. https://doi.org/10.4135/9781071886229.n151

Chapter 11, EMPOWER Students with Authority and Responsibility

1. Erwin, J. (2004). *The classroom of choice: Giving students what they need and getting what you want* (pp. 14-15). Association for Supervision and Curriculum Development.

2. Glasser, W. (1999). *Choice theory* pp. 25-43). Harper Perennial.

3. Erwin, J. (2004). *The classroom of choice: Giving students what they need and getting what you want.* Association for Supervision and Curriculum Development.

Chapter 12, EMPOWER Students with Meaningful Learning

1. Prochnau, W. (1990, May.) Last stand for the old woods. *Life* (pp. 52-60).

2. Bryce, T.G.K., & Brown, E. J. (2023, April 26). Ausubel's meaningful learning revisited. *Current Psychology, 43.* doi.org/10.1007/s12144-023-04440-4

3. CLRN Team. (2025, April 8). *What is meaningful learning?* California Learning Research Network. https://www.clrn.org/what-is-meaningful-learning/

   Jones., E. W. (2025). *Ausubel's theory of meaningful learning.* PsychologyFor. https://psychologyfor.com/ausubels-theory-of-meaningful-learning/

4. Prinrski, S. J., Hecht, C. A., & Harackiewicz, J. M. (2017, October 18). Making learning personally meaningful: A new framework for relevance research. *Journal of Experiential Education 86(1), 11-29.*

5. Prinrski, S. J., Hecht, C. A., & Harackiewicz, J. M. (2017, October 18). Making learning personally meaningful: A new framework for relevance research. *Journal of Experiential Education* 86(1), 11-29.

6. Kembler, D., Ho, A., & Hong, C. (2008, November 1). The importance of establishing relevance in motivating student learning. *Active Learning in Higher Education.* (9)3, 249-263. https://doi.org/10.1177/1469787408095

Chapter 13, EMPOWER Students with Challenge and Success

1. Vygotsky, L.S. (1997). *Educational Psychology.* CRC Press. https://doi.org/10.4324/9780429273070
    McLeod, S. (2025, October 16). *Vygotsky's theory of cognitive development.* SimplyPsychology. https://www.simplypsychology.org/vygotsk

2. Toth, M. D. & Sousa, D. A. (2019). *The power of student teams: Achieving social, emotional, and cognitive learning in every classroom through academic teaming* (p. 12). Learning Sciences International.

3. Science Direct. (2026). *Attribution theory.* https://www.sciencedirect.com/topics/social-sciences/attribution-theory

4. Dweck, C. S., Walton, G. M., & Cohen, G. L. (2014). *Academic tenacity: Mindsets and skills that promote long-term learning.* Bill & Melinda Gates Foundation. https://ed.stanford.edu/sites/default/files/manual/dweck-walton-cohen-2014.pdf

5. Acevedo, S. (2020, October 21). F.A.I.L.= "First attempt in learning." Stanford Technology Ventures Program. https://stvp.stanford.edu/clips/f-a-i-l-first-attempt-in-learning/

6. Phillips, D. (2025, July 16). *Giving students time and confidence to build their metacognition skills* (paras. 16-19). Edutopia. https://www.edutopia.org/article/boosting-students-metacognition-skills

7. Fogarty, R., & Pete, B. (2020). *Metacognition: The neglected skill set for empowering students.* The Solution Tree.

8. California Learning Research Network (2025, July 2), *Why is metacognition so important for learning and memory?* CLRN. https://www.clrn.org/why-is-metacognition-so-important-for-learning-and-memory/

Stanton, J.D., Sebesta, A.J., & Dunlosky, J. (2021). Fostering metacognition to support student learning and performance. *CBE Life Science Education, 20*(2). https://pubmed.ncbi.nlm.nih.gov/33797282/

9. Hattie, J. (2023). *Visible learning: The sequel* (pp. 85-86). Routledge.

Chapter 14, EMPOWER Students with Self-Reflection and Self-Evaluation

1. Price-Mitchell, M. (2020, October 9). What is metacognition? How does it help us think? Metacognitive strategies like self-reflection empower students for a lifetime. *Psychology Today.* https://www.psychologytoday.com/us/blog/the-moment-youth/202010/what-is-metacognition-how-does-it-help-us-think

2. Kinney, P. (2012). *Fostering student accountability through student-led conferences.* Association for Middle Level Education and National Association of Secondary School Principals.

Chapter 15, EMPOWER Students with Technology

1. Meriam-Webster Dictionary. (2026). *Technology.* https://www.merriam-webster.com/dictionary/technology

2. California Learning Resource Network. (2025, July 2). *Why should technology be used in the classroom?* CLRN. https://www.clrn.org/why-should-technology-be-used-in-the-classroom/
    Tabassum, N. (2025, May). *The use of technology in the classroom: A review of best practices.* ResearchGate. DOI:10.13140/RG.2.2.29626.71364

3. Doss, C. J., Bozick, R., Schwartz, H. L., Chu, L., Rainey, L. R., Woo, A., Reich, J. & Dukes, J. (2025, September 30). *AI use in schools is quickly increasing but guidance lags behind.* RAND. https://www.rand.org/pubs/research_reports/RRA4180-1.html

4. Bowen, J.A., & Watson, C.E. (2025). *Teaching with AI: A practical guide to a new era of human learning,* 2nd Edition, Johns Hopkins University Press.
    Burns, M. (2024). *Ed tech essentials: 12 strategies for every classroom in the age of AI, 2nd Edition.* Association for Supervision and Curriculum Development.

Center for Reinventing Public Education. (2026). *AI and education policy 101: The evolving landscape and examples from early adopters.* https://crpe.org/ai-and-education-policy-101-the-evolving-landscape-and-examples-from-early-adopters;

Frontier, T. (2025). *AI with intention: Principles and action steps for teachers and school leaders.* Association for Supervision and Curriculum Development.

5. American Academy of Child & Adolescent Psychiatry. (2025, June). *Screen time and children.* AACAP. https://www.aacap.org/AACAP/Families_and_Youth/Facts_for_Families/FFF-Guide/Children-And-Watching-TV-054.aspx

6. EdTechRSE. (2026). *What percentage of schools use technology in the classroom? You'll be surprised!* ETR. https://edtechrce.org/what-percentage-of-schools-use-technology-in-the-classroom/

7. American Psychological Association. (2025, June 9). *Screen time and emotional problems in kids: A vicious circle?* APA. https://www.apa.org/news/press/releases/2025/06/screen-time-problems-children
Zablotsky B, Ng, A. E., Black, L. I., Haile, G., Bose, J., Jones, J.R., Blumberg, P. D. (2025). Associations between screen time use and health outcomes among US teenagers. *Preventing Chronic Disease (22)*8, 1-11. https://www.cdc.gov/pcd/issues/2025/pdf/24_0537.pdf

8. Andoh, E. (2025, October 1). *Many teens are turning to AI chatbots for friendship and emotional support.* American Psychological Association. https://www.apa.org/monitor/2025/10/technology-youth-friendships
Chatterjee, R. (2025, September 19). *Their teenage sons died by suicide. Now, they are sounding an alarm about AI chatbots.* National Public Radio.
https://www.npr.org/sections/shots-health-news/2025/09/19/nx-s1-5545749/ai-chatbots-safety-openai-meta-characterai-teens-suicide
Examining the Harm of AI Chatbots. (2025, September 1). Written Testimony from Matthew Raine, Father of Adam Raine, Before the United States Senate Judiciary Subcommittee on Crime and Counterterrorism, September 16, 2025
https://www.judiciary.senate.gov/imo/media/doc/e2e8fc50-a9ac-05ec-edd7-277cb0afcdf2/2025-09-16%20PM%20-%20Testimony%20-%20Raine.pdf

Goedecke, S. (2025, April 28). *Sycophancy is the first LLM "dark pattern"*. Sean Goedecke, Australian software engineer, expert opinion piece. https://www.seangoedecke.com/ai-sycophancy/
Payne, K. (2024, October 25). *An AI chatbot pushed a teen to kill himself, a lawsuit against its creator alleges*. Associated Press News. https://apnews.com/article/chatbot-ai-lawsuit-suicide-teen-artificial-intelligence-9d48adc572100822fdbc3c90d1456bd0

9. Mayo Clinic. (2024, June 19). *Screen time and children*. https://www.mayoclinic.org/healthy-lifestyle/childrens-health/in-depth/screen-time/art-20047952

10. American Academy of Pediatrics. (2025, March 13). *Screen time at school*. AAP. https://www.aap.org/en/patient-care/media-and-children/center-of-excellence-on-social-media-and-youth-mental-health/qa-portal/qa-portal-library/qa-portal-library-questions/screen-time-at-school/

Acknowledgments

John F. Kennedy reminds us, "We must find time to stop and thank the people who make a difference in our lives," and so we do. There are far too many people to list who helped us frame, reframe, write, rewrite, organize, and reorganize this manuscript, but we especially want to acknowledge the tremendous help given to us by the following individuals:

The "silent" author of this book has been our editor, **Marj Frank.** As with our other books, she guided, encouraged, and challenged us from start to finish. She expanded our thinking, searched out research to validate our thoughts, added her own valuable perspectives, and kept us on track to finish. Our most sincere thanks and appreciation go out to this amazing editor and friend.

We are grateful to our friend and colleague **Tom Murray** for crafting such a thoughtful foreword. It is an honor that this award-winning author and speaker took time from his busy schedule to review our work and share such kind words about it.

As with our previous books, we again extend our gratitude to our friend and colleague **Rick Wormeli.** When he learned we were working on a new project, he generously offered to review it and devoted valuable time from other commitments to provide thoughtful, honest, and constructive feedback that strengthened our work.

Several friends and colleagues shared examples and stories with us to support the power of expecting, engaging, and empowering.

Thanks to Alex Aiken, Jen Bolton, Justin Bolton, Paul Destino, Linda Hilligoss, Julie Reynolds, and Nanci Strickland for sharing their experiences with us.

Our experience with these concepts was drawn from work with, among so many others, **Ashland Middle School** and **Talent Middle School** in Oregon (Patti), and **the Coweta County School System** in Georgia and the **Evergreen School District** in Montana (Laurie). The staff, students, and families from these schools provided us with much of the knowledge, background, and understanding of just how important the concepts of expecting more, engaging more, and empowering more are, all of which improve student learning.

A book simply cannot be written without the support of **family and friends**. Thank you all for understanding and putting up with the numerous hours spent writing that pulled us away from spending time with each of you. We give special thanks to our husbands **Daniel Eugene Barron** and **Daniel Eugene Bolton** (can you believe they even have the same name?) for all their support along the way. We also want to give a shout out to Laurie's daughter, **Emma Barron** (now a college graduate), for her continued support and contributions.

About the Authors

Laurie and Patti both have the distinguished honor of being named NASSP National Middle Level Principals of the Year (Patti in 2003 and Laurie in 2013). Though a decade separates their honors, they both agree that holding high expectations and engaging and empowering students are the true keys to student learning.

Together, Laurie and Patti have co-authored *The Successful Middle School: A Place to Belong and Become, 2nd Edition, We Belong: 50 Strategies to Create Community and Revolutionize Classroom Management, Middle School: A Place to Belong and Become*, and *What Parents Need to Know about Common Core and Other College- and Career-Ready Standards.*

Dr. Laurie Barron is in her 31st year in education, with experience as a high school English teacher, middle school assistant principal, and middle school principal. Since 2013, she has served as the superintendent of the Evergreen School District in Kalispell, Montana.

Laurie holds a BSEd in English Education from the University of Georgia, an MEd in Supervision and Administration from the University of West Georgia, and an EdS and EdD in Educational Leadership from the University of Sarasota. She studied abroad at Oxford University, holds National Superintendent Certification, and is a National Board Certified Teacher. She was honored as Teacher of the Year, STAR Teacher, the 2012 Georgia Middle School Principal of the Year, and the 2013 National Middle School Principal of the Year.

Laurie was also named the 2019 Empowered Superintendent of the Year by the Montana Educational Technologists Association and is the 2021 and 2026 Montana Superintendent of the Year. In 2022, Barron received the Distinguished Alumni Lifetime Achievement Award from the University of Georgia College of Education. Laurie has also authored numerous articles in multiple educational publications.

A national and international speaker, consultant, and leadership coach, Laurie focuses on student belonging, engagement, school culture, instructional practices, and leadership development.

Laurie is living the dream in Montana with her husband Daniel and their rescue puppy Willy, where together they enjoy spending time in their off grid cabin, watching Georgia Bulldogs football, snow skiing, rafting, hiking, camping, and enjoying time with their three adult daughters.

Connect with Laurie: @LaurieBarron on X, lauriebarron-7015b45b on LinkedIn, or lauriebarron18@gmail.com

Patti Kinney decided in first grade to become a teacher—initially because she wanted to be "the person who told kids what to do," though she soon learned the job meant far more than that. She began as an elementary music specialist before teaching fifth through seventh grades and later serving as assistant principal and principal of Talent Middle School. Under her leadership, the school became one of NASSP's "100 Highly Successful Middle Schools."

A past president of both the Association for Middle Level Education and the Oregon Middle Level Association, Patti has received numerous honors, including Oregon Assistant Principal of the Year (1996), Oregon Principal of the Year (2002), and MetLife/NASSP National Middle Level Principal of the Year (2003). She also received Southern Oregon University's Excellence in Education Award and has an OMLA Distinguished Service Award named in her honor.

From 2007–2014, Patti served as Associate Director for Middle Level Services at NASSP. She continues to speak, write, and consult primarily on middle level education worldwide. Patti holds degrees from Southern Oregon University and the University of Oregon. She and her husband, Dan Bolton, live in Cottage Grove, Oregon—where their story together began in first grade.

Connect with Patti: kinneypatti@gmail.com, @pckinney on X, or Kinney Patti on LinkedIn

More from
ConnectEDD Publishing

Since 2015, ConnectEDD has worked to transform education by empowering educators to become better-equipped to teach, learn, and lead. What started as a small company designed to provide professional learning events for educators has grown to include a variety of services to help educators and administrators address essential challenges. ConnectEDD offers instructional and leadership coaching, professional development workshops focusing on a variety of educational topics, a roster of nationally recognized educator associates who possess hands-on knowledge and experience, educational conferences custom-designed to meet the specific needs of schools, districts, and state/national organizations, and ongoing, personalized support, both virtually and onsite. In 2020, ConnectEDD expanded to include publishing services designed to provide busy educators with books and resources consisting of practical information on a wide variety of teaching, learning, and leadership topics. Please visit us online at connecteddpublishing.com or contact us at: info@connecteddpublishing.com

Recent Publications:

Live Your Excellence: Action Guide by Jimmy Casas

Culturize: Action Guide by Jimmy Casas

Daily Inspiration for Educators: Positive Thoughts for Every Day of the Year by Jimmy Casas

Eyes on Culture: Multiply Excellence in Your School by Emily Paschall

Pause. Breathe. Flourish. Living Your Best Life as an Educator by William D. Parker

L.E.A.R.N.E.R. Finding the True, Good, and Beautiful in Education by Marita Diffenbaugh

Educator Reflection Tips Volume II: Refining Our Practice by Jami Fowler-White

Handle With Care: Managing Difficult Situations in Schools with Dignity and Respect by Jimmy Casas and Joy Kelly

Disruptive Thinking: Preparing Learners for Their Future by Eric Sheninger

Permission to be Great: Increasing Engagement in Your School by Dan Butler

Daily Inspiration for Educators: Positive Thoughts for Every Day of the Year, Volume II by Jimmy Casas

The 6 Literacy Levers: Creating a Community of Readers by Brad Gustafson

The Educator's ATLAS: Your Roadmap to Engagement by Weston Kieschnick

In This Season: Words for the Heart by Todd Nesloney, LaNesha Tabb, Tanner Olson, and Alice Lee

Leading with a Humble Heart: A 40-Day Devotional for Leaders by Zac Bauermaster

Recalibrate the Culture: Our Why…Our Work…Our Values by Jimmy Casas

Creating Curious Classrooms: The Beauty of Questions by Emma Chiappetta

Crafting the Culture: 45 Reflections on What Matters Most by Joe Sanfelippo and Jeffrey Zoul

Improving School Mental Health: The Thriving School Community Solution by Charle Peck and Dr. Cameron Caswell

Building Authenticity: A Blueprint for the Leader Inside You by Todd Nesloney and Tyler Cook

Connecting Through Conversation: A Playbook for Talking with Students by Erika Bare and Tiffany Burns

The Dream Factory: Designing a Purposeful Life by Mark Trumbo

Stories Behind Stances: Creating Empathy Through Hearing "The Other Side" by Chris Singleton

Happy Eyes: Becoming All Things to All People by Ryan Tillman

The Generative Age: Artificial Intelligence and the Future of Education by Alana Winnick

Recalibrate the Culture: Action Guide by Jimmy Casas

Leading with PEOPLE: A Six Pillar Framework for Fruitful Leadership by Zac Bauermaster

A School Leader's Guide to Reclaiming Purpose by Frederick C. Buskey

Foundations of an Elite Culture: Building Success with High Standards and a Positive Environment by David Arencibia

Personalize: Meeting the Needs of All Learners by Eric Sheninger and Nicki Slaugh

The Five Principles of Educator Professionalism: Rebuilding Trust in Schools by Nason Lollar

Words on the Wall: Culturizing Your Classroom For Observable Impact by Jimmy Casas and Cale Birk

School of Engagement: 45 Activities to Ignite Student Learning by Jonathan Alsheimer

Intentional Instructional Moves: Strategic Steps to Accelerate Student Learning by Sherry St. Clair

Overcoming Education: Complex Challenges, Difficult People, and the Art of Making a Difference by Brad R. Gustafson

The Language of Behavior: A Framework to Elevate Student Success by Charle Peck and Joshua Stamper

Whose Permission Are You Waiting For? An Educator's Guide to Doing What You Love by William D. Parker

The Leader You're Not…And Why It's Just As Important As the Leader You Are by Scott Borba

The Growth-Minded Leader by Tyler Cook

Day by Day: 180 Days of Hope and Encouragement by Zac Bauermaster

Make Your Move: For Ambitious People Ready to Live Their Aspirations by Marlon Styles, Jr.

The Hidden Work: What Separates Top Performers From Underachievers by Weston Kieschnick

Lifted to Lead: How a Paraplegic Orphan Rose from the Streets of Saigon to Become an American Leader by Stefan Bean and Kathy Nash

Lead From Who You Are: The Personal, People, and Process Rhythms of Meaningful Leadership by Joe Sanfelippo

Ready to Lead with AI: A Practical Guide for School Leaders by Kip Glazer

When All Means All: The Constellation of Learning Approach to Student-Centered Schools by Adam D. Drummond-Konopasek and Danny Drummond-Konopasek

A School Leader's Playbook for Tough Conversations by Erika Bare and Tiffany Burns